A HISTORY O

by

The Reverend F W Cleverdon,
Rector of Mells 1959-1969

The Frome Society for Local Study

First published by the Frome Society for Local Study 1974
Second edition   "   "   "   "   "   2003
Third revised edition "   "   "   "   "   2014

Printed by Harrier LLC

ISBN 978-0-9565869-8-8

*Rev Francis Cleverdon checking source material for his
History of Mells in 1974*
Courtesy of *The Somerset Standard.*

CONTENTS

PREFACE

Over several years I have collected odd bits of information about Mells, and I am not always able to give the source of an item. To overcome the problem I thought it better to give a list of the many publications from which my information is drawn. I owe a great deal to the many publications of the Somerset Record Society and the Somerset Archaeological Society, to Collinson's, Page's, Phelps', and the Victoria Histories of Somerset and Wiltshire, and Somerset and Dorset Notes and Queries. I have also drawn on Wickham's Spade and Terrier, Old Mendip by Robert Atthill, The Woollen Industry of South-West England by K G Ponting, and The History of the Somerset Coalfield by C G Down and A J Warrington.

I am grateful to Mrs Raymond Asquith who made it possible for me to read the various MSS dealing with the Manor and the Horner family,* and latterly to the Earl of Oxford and Asquith who has allowed me access to the records of the Court Leet and Court Baron of the Liberty and Manor of Mells and Leigh. As Rector I had access to the Parish Chest with all its records and the records of the Court Baron of the Manor and Rectory of Mells cum Leigh. Rev Geo Horner (1875-1891) did much research among the Glastonbury Abbey MSS at Longleat and some information is from his notes. Other valuable material came from the memoirs of former residents, Mr Richard White, born at Holwell Farm in 1828, and the Long family of the firm of masons and plasterers who carried on business in Mells for more than a century. Thanks to Mr A J S White and Mrs Percy Osborne (née Long) I have been able to use these memoirs. Finally, I should like to thank Mr Michael McGarvie, Honorary Secretary of the Frome Society for Local Study, for his interest and advice, and Mrs Lilian Maggs for reading the proofs.

*MSS in the Manor:
Memoirs of the Family of Horner of Mells AB (c1740)
Records of the Horner Family, Sir Herbert Jekyll 1482-1932
Catalogue of Horner MSS. 1280-1833
St Andrew's College Diary.

INTRODUCTION TO THE THIRD EDITION

'A History of Mells' by Rev Francis Cleverdon was first published by the Frome Society for Local Study (FSLS) in 1974; a second edition with minor alterations was published in 2003. Although it must now be regarded as a period piece, it has proved so popular that FSLS is now publishing a third edition. Michael McGarvie edited the previous editions and I would like to thank him for his advice and guidance.

I am most grateful to the Earl and Countess of Oxford and Asquith for their interest and help and wish to thank Lord Oxford for correcting a number of errors in the text of the previous editions and for his permission to reproduce several paintings by WW Wheatley and other photographs. I also wish to thank Peter Lowry for permission to use his photographs of Mells that appeared in the earlier editions and to other people who lent photographs which appear in the new edition.

Alan Yeates has improved many of the illustrations and is responsible for the presentation and layout of the book. The index has been revised to make it more valuable and a short bibliography has been added. Richard White's memoirs were published in 1990 by FSLS as 'Memoirs of a Victorian Farmer' and the recollections of AB appeared in the FSLS Yearbook Volume 1 in 1987. Those readers who wish to learn more about the Fussells, are referred to 'Men of Iron- the Fussells of Mells' by Robin Thornes, published by FSLS in 2010.

Alastair MacLeay June 2014

St Andrews Church, Mells   *Tom Horner*

IN THE BEGINNING

Ian Kiel, in *The Garden of Glastonbury*[1], gives the following particulars of the produce of the Abbey garden sent to Mells: Cider, "two tuns, for the Abbot's use whilst staying there." Pears: "One bushel was sent for the Abbot's use at Mells." He goes on to say: "Mells, to which provisions were sent, was a manor on the main route from Glastonbury to Oxford and London, and it was a regular stopping place for travellers on abbey business to and from Wiltshire and beyond."

The importance of Mells to the abbey travellers is obvious when we remember that it was the most easterly of the abbey's possessions, which stretched from Mells on the north east, to the right bank of the river Parrett, on the south west, an area comprising one eighth of the County of Somerset, and containing one tenth of its population.[2]

It is hundreds of thousands of years ago that the physical character of Mells took shape during what has been called the Mendip Upheaval. "The coal strata have not only been raised to a vertical position, but have actually been folded back upon themselves, so that instead of dipping northwards from the Mendip hills they now dip southwards towards the range." This upheaval left the rift which cuts the village in half, and runs under the Tor at Vobster, through Melcombe and the Iron Valley, and also the rift which forms the eastern boundary of the Parish, Whatley Bottom and Murdercombe.

Ancient camps surround the village: Tedbury, Wadbury, Newbury and Kingsdown. On Tedbury have been found querns (hand mills), one of which is in Frome Museum, British implements and implements of war, and also coins of the Roman emperors. Flints can still be found on this site. In the village there are such martial names as Tents Hill and Drums Hill. Tents Hill is mentioned as early as 1678.

The earliest mention of Mells is in the Saxon Charter.

King Edmund granted the manor to the Earl Athelstan in 942. The Earl gave the manor to Glastonbury Abbey, and so in the Domesday Book we read that: "The Church itself holds Mylle."

Leland, who visited Mells soon after the dissolution of the monastery, states that: "There is a praty Maner Place of Stone harde at the Weste Ende of the Chirche." He goes on to say: "This be likelihood was partly buildid by Abbate Selwoode of Glasteinbyre. Syns it servid the Fermer of the Lordship."

The Manor would have been well used and served as the Guest House for the more important visitors. When Bishop Saveric made his successful attempt to become the Abbot of Glastonbury it was from Mells that he issued anathema against William (Pica), as rival abbot, and laid an interdict upon the monastery. The appointment of Saveric as both Bishop of Wells and abbot was one of the conditions laid down by Henry VI, Holy Roman Emperor, for the release of Richard I from prison.[3]

The abbots would, as Lords of the Manor, visit Mells at least once a year to collect their rents and other dues from their tenants. It was probably for this occasion that the two tuns of cider and one bushel of pears were sent.

As Glastonbury was a popular place for pilgrimages there would always be many coming and going and passing through Mells. The presence of so many clothiers in the Mendip area also meant that there was a great deal of coming and going between this part of Somerset and London. Clothiers were capitalists "who bought and owned the wool, but had all the work, except the fulling, done at the worker's home, the implements being owned by the workers themselves."[4] Leland tells us that Mells was "a praty Townlet of Clothing" and goes on to say that Abbot Selwood was impressed "by the welthiness there of the people." He points out that the Vestry was built largely through the generosity of "one Garland, a draper of London." The coat of arms on the outer wall of the vestry is probably that of a Tailors' Company; a tent between two parliamentary robes. Among the famous clothiers of Somerset "were the Sharlands of Mells where they are known as London Merchants."[5] In 1685, Henry Cornish, a former sheriff of London, was executed. He carried on a clothing business in Mells in a house which stood on the site of the present Rectory.[6]

The evolution of the means of travel between Mells and London has been great, and by the time the weaving industry was on the wane, was becoming much easier. In 1739, Joseph Clavey was proprietor of the Flying Wagon, i e a coach to London. The coach left Frome on Monday, 1 a m and arrived at The King's Arms, Holborn at 12 noon on Wednesday. The return journey was made on Thursday, leaving at 1 o'clock and arriving in Frome at 12 noon on Saturday.[7] Joseph Clavey was probably the son of Abraham Clavey, of Mells, who was described as a carrier in 1709. The abortive Dorset and Somerset Canal, which ran along the northern boundary of the Parish, was near completion when the railway arrived in 1851, and by 1858 Mells had its own station at Mells Road.

The Churchwardens' accounts tell of another kind of coming and going. In 1673 the bellringers were paid "for ringing ye Bishop through Towne, 5/8." Bridgwater (and probably other Bristol Channel ports) landed many travellers who were to pass through Mells.

1663: "gave several poor traviling men and women £1-2-8." 1673: "Pd. for many Poore distressed Sea Passengers being taken by the Dutch and set on shore whos Names appeare by particulars, 18/-"
1683: "Given to ffrench protestant gent and his wife, 5/-."
1688: "Gave several passengers having Justices of the peace hands to their Certificates, £2-11-6." "Gave a soldier whose arm was shot off 3d." "To 42 soldiers and passengers 7/5."
1701: "Gave to seamen who had their ship castaway, 8d."
1717: "Gave a soldier on his journey home, 1/-."

From this it can be seen that Mells was indeed a main route to and from Wiltshire and beyond.

[1] S A S, 104, 1333/4

[2] V H S, 2, 85

[3] C H S, 11, 252

[4] Ponting, 130

[5] S A S, 39, 23

[6] A B, FSLS Yearbook 1, 1987

[7] Bath Chronicle, 1745

DOMESDAY

The Domesday Book gives the following account of Mells: "The Church itself holds Mylle. Alnod the abbot held it and T R E (the time of King Edward) it paid geld for 20 hides. There is land for 20 ploughs. Of this (land) there is in demesne of 10 hides where are 2 ploughs and 2 serfs and (there are) 8 villeins and 7 bordars and 5 cottars with 3 ploughs and 3½ hides. There are 1 riding horse and 7 beasts and 15 swine and 100 sheep less 9. There is a mill paying 5 shillings and 15 acres of meadow and 12 acres of pasture. Woodland 1 league long and 2 furlongs broad. It is worth 10 pounds to the abbot. And when Turstin received it, 100 shillings. Of the land of the manor Godeve holds of the abbot 1 hide. Her Husband (vir ejus) held (it) T R E, nor could it be separated from the church. It is worth 78 pence."[1]

The serf was a bondman and did the meaner tasks in the village. Villeins were small farmers, and bordars and cottars were labourers. All did homage to the lord of the manor, but over the years each class got more freedom, and by the reign of Edward I there remained few slaves.

The lord of the manor would hold his land under the king and had obligations to him. One of these was to provide, as the need arose, men for the army. There was knight's service which the lord provided, and there were in Mells the "able men to serve the king." In Abbot Selwood's time there were "able to do the king service to the nombre of 30. Also there be in the same lordship certaine bondmen to the nombre of 1."[2]

In a Certificate of Musters, dated 1569, the following particulars are given of the duties of the able men. John Godfrey, Thos Lane, John Coles, John Badell and John Rusdon were pikemen, Wm James, an archer, Wm Prattant, a gonner, and John Martyn, a billman. In addition there was "one tithing corslet furnished." Wm Orange provided a corslet furnished and Stephen Cabell, a bow, a sheaf of arrows, a skull and a bill. John Truckwell and Robert Norman were down for 2 bows and 2 sheaves of arrows. Margerie Cottynton possessed a corslet furnished, one harquebut, a bow, a sheaf of arrows and a skull.[3] Three corslets, or suits of armour, suggest that the parish had to supply equipment for three knights. 1569 was after the dissolution of Glastonbury Abbey and shows the lord's obligations remained as they were before that event.

The militia was a development from this and Oldmixon says "that in 1642 Sir John Horner commanded the Somerset Militia and armed his servants and retainers. His memory and merits do honour his name." In this case they were not used for the king but for parliament. In later years the armed forces were provided out of taxation, but when Napoleon threatened these shores with invasion there were two companies of the Frome Selwood Volunteers in Mells. "Colonel Horner spent much money in finishing Mells Park House and on the North Somerset Yeomanry which made it necessary for him to live at Weymouth."[4]

The 20 hides mentioned in Domesday could have been the common lands: the eastfields and the westfields. There were no hedges as there are now; indeed we are told that as late as 1678 "there was hardly a hedge between the Churchyards of Mells and Babington."[5]

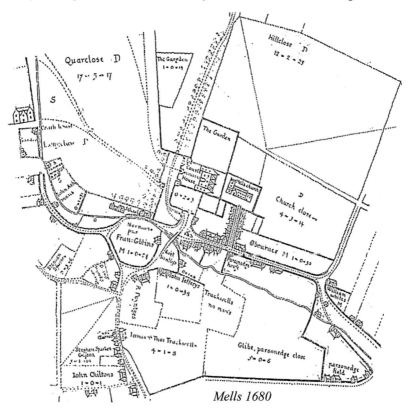

Mells 1680

13

Woodlands End may give a clue to the woodland. It could have extended from Woodlands End through the valley to Vobster. It is known that there were a large number of well grown oaks in the present park. In Spade and Terrier, Rev J Wickham says that: "Fine oaks abound in the district. A specimen which measures 22 feet round at 6 feet from the ground, stands close to Mells House." In 1314 John Samuel held 20 acres of wood and 100 acres of heath.[6] There are several accounts in the records of oaks being used for the repairs of the church. In 1759 "for haleing a oak from Melcom to the Church, 7/-", "digging a Sawpit in Melcom and filling it up, 2/6."

The mill mentioned in Domesday was at the Duckery, Wrags Mill as it was called. It is first mentioned in 1554. In 1769 there was an agreement "between William Brown, of Mells, miller, on the one part, and Thomas Horner of the same, esquire, of the other part, for the exchange of a house and mill called Wrags Mill in Mells for a tenement called Bilboa in Mells." Wrags Mill was the Manor Mill, and the lord of the manor had the sole right of milling. But there were encroachments on his preserves. In 1637 Nicholas Fuller, of Mells, was granted a licence "to buy 5 quarters of whete, Rye and barley weekly, and to convert into Meale, and sell the same within the Parishe of Mells aforesaid."

He was not alone, for in 1661 the question of the manor rights was raised in court "on the question whether any toll or multure due to a certain water mill, being the ancient custom of the manor of Mells." Five querns for malt had been erected in Mells within 20 years to the damage of the manor mill. "Moreover they had deceived the people, in regard that the malt made less beer,- for the corns are broken not ground."[7] The Duckery Cottages took on their present pseudo-Gothic character after the closure of the old mill. All that remains of the mill at Bilboa are some ruins at the west of the house. Two Derby millstones remain, one buried under a recent fall of masonry and the other at Charnwood on the Green. The mill closed down just before the Second World War.

[1] V H S, 1, 465
[2] C H S, 2, 463
[3] S R S, 20, 298, 1904 A skull was a type of close fitting helmet
[4] Jekyll
[5] A B
[6] Feet of Fines, S R S, XII, 39, 49,1898
[7] V H S, 11, 402

THE LIBERTY AND MANOR
OF MELLS AND LEIGH

(a) Court Leet

It is on record that the Bishop claimed the Liberty of Mells in 1254. A liberty is the offshoot of a Hundred, in this case of Kilmersdon,[1] and is free to manage its own affairs under the sovereign. Every manor had its Court Baron but Mells had its Court Leet. "The Court Leet is the most ancient tribunal of the Common Law, and derives its authority from the Crown."[2] It elected the Constable, the Tythingman, and the Hayward for the Liberty.

The Court Baron dealt with estate management and protected the rights of the Lord of the Manor and the tenants in Mells. The two courts appear to have met together and to have been an all-powerful Parish Council dealing with all the public services with the exception of the care of the poor, which was the responsibility of the Vestry.

Within the Manor of Mells and Leigh there were four other lesser manors, the Rectorial Manor of Mells cum Leigh, Samuels, Haydon and Frenchouse. All held their separate courts. These were not compact estates or farms, as we might expect, but consisted of tenements and holdings in several parts of the Manor. A survey of the Rectory in 1638 states: "There doth belong to the Parsonage of Mells a manner and the Tenants there do hold by copy of Court usage, and there are six in Mells and nine in Leigh."

A 1678 survey of Mells suggests that Samuels House was just north of the Manor House. Frenchouse is the present Branch Farm, once called Vranch Farm. These two manors were purchased by the Horner family, but still held separate courts. It is not clear when these courts ceased to exist.

The last recorded Court Leet and Court Baron for the Manor was in 1831, but the last recorded Court Baron for the Rectory was 1843. By this time the Select Vestry had assumed responsibility for Parish affairs and was to be followed in 1894 by the Parish Council.

All the Court records we have follow the Commonwealth period. Sir John Horner, a Parliamentarian, died in 1659. The confusion of the period on the estate is reflected in the records of the Court Leet. It is not surprising that one of the first things the Court had to deal with was certain irregularities which had been allowed during the period of the

The Blind House   *A R Yeates*

Commonwealth. One item concerns "an information of wrongs and Trespasses done and committed against the Right Worshipful Sir George Horner Kt, by several of his tenants upon his Manner in and about Mells." Two brothers had "sold many sacks of cole on the marsh your worshipp having no share thereof." It is now 1665, "and since the decease of your father your worshipp have lost out of the Lordship of Mells three hundred loads of Tymber thereabouts."

It is interesting to recall how much power was in the hands of the local people in the past. Weights and measures were the responsibility of the bailiff. There were at one time as many as three millards, five virtualers (victuallers), four bakers, six alehousekeepers and five "foreign" bakers. Constant reference is made to the duty of weighing the bread, "once a month" or even "once a week". Apparently the Constable got so upset in 1798 about the state of affairs that he attempted to call the Jury together himself to discuss the matter, and failing, he called in the Constable of Kilmersdon to check the parish weights and measures. The Court's answer to this was: "Now we present the same was illegal and that no other Constable of any Manor or Liberty or Parish has any authority in this Liberty."

"Loose and idle" persons were reported for not taking to themselves some service. There was great concern throughout the whole of the 18th century about the prison house, stocks, pillory, whipping post and ducking stool. No one did anything about them. Yet the court is continually presenting that they must be restored as they were before. Sometimes the Lord of the Manor is ordered to do it, sometimes the Rector and sometimes the Constable. It may be the Court did not know who was responsible and so no one responded to its order. The Blind House remains to show that someone did at last rebuild the prison, but there is no record as to who it was. There were also breaches of the law to be dealt with. In 1704 one Thomas Hort was presented for "keeping a kittle alley being unlawful game and to leave the same upon paine of five shillings."

Other matters included persons who allowed "their pigs to run about the fields without spanning, yoaking and ringing," the keeping of ducks "which was an anoyance to the waters," persons "who make dung hills in the street," and John Smith, of Leigh, "for washing the Bellies and Insides of Cattle in the Water Course of Leigh aforesaid and fowling the same to the prejudice and anoyance of the inhabitants." Or, "Richard Poyntz and Thomas Huntley for setting House Offices on the watercourse." Neighbourly differences were also settled: "We present ye well called Egypt well lying in ye widow Hodynots backside to be an accustomed well for ye neighbouring tenants to egress and regress without any let or hindrance."

The highways, church paths, bridle paths, and market ways were the responsibility of the parishioners and therefore of the Court. "We present the Town Brig and Berry Brig to be mended by the waywardens." "We present the Supervisor of Mells for not repairing the way from finger to Mells and also haydon, supposing to be ye market way to frome called fursey lane. Also the way from Mells Little Green and haydon in ye lane called Hoely Lane out of repair." "We present that the market way is stopt between coleford and the finger." Although New Street had been built for more than 200 years in 1672, "We present that we cannot by our view on new street, but that it is well at present, and cannot find Whether it ought to bee mended by the parish or by the tenants"

The waywardens and private individuals were alike guilty of quarrying stone from wherever they could. The Court dealt with it in this way: "We likewise present ye Waywardens for digging in ye fore mentioned Quar on ye Green and not making provision to fill it in again."

The watercourses, the small streams and road gutters, came under their jurisdiction. They declared: "The watercourse to be defective between the Conduit and the shoot at the town brig," the Town Bridge being the bridge at the bottom of Limekiln Hill. The watercourses were the care of the owners and tenants who "do Injoy ye lands on both sides," and in tips particular case those who occupied the "plowlands Lying in the Common fields of Mells."

During the Commonwealth period a number of cottages were built on the Lord's land. "We present cottages built . . ., an inclosure made by George Yeomans adjoining the widdow garlands ground. And they are to pull down their cottages and lay open their inclosure between this and the next Court." There were many encroachments of the Lord's waste and land. A strange one was in 1767 when the Court declared that: "Mr Thomas Bridges Senr, to have encroacht on Mr Horners Royalty by planting a row of ashen trees from holy Bush to Leigh." As late as 1827 the court indicted "James West of the Parish of Leigh, Labourer, at a place called Whitehold bounding on Carlstone Wood who has inclosed a piece of ground there and converted it to a garden."

The open field system appears to have survived until the beginning of the 18th Century. The Park House was built in 1740 and the Park enclosed as we know it now. In 1720 Charity Land rented to the Horners is referred to as recently enclosed in the Churchwardens' Records. A possible reference to enclosures is mentioned in the Court Rolls of 1665. Sir George made his home in Mells, and it would appear that he enclosed land around the Manor House "also The Parke at Mells, the sheep sleight upon heydon for fourscore sheepe. Arable land in both fields." The process could have been a gradual one for the Court gave liberty to Phillip Payne in 1678 "to inclose four acres on Mendip in Normans Dole."

(b) Court Baron

The management of the estate was the chief concern of the Court Baron. The copy holder was usually head of the family. He would hold his estate for life, if married his widow would hold it for her life, and then it would pass to the next life; often the son. As each person died so a new life was added to the lease. In this way a family could hold a lease for several generations. The Lord of the Manor's income came from the sale of the copyhold in the first instance, and then from rents and from heriots paid at the death of each tenant. The rent was very little, perhaps

6/8 for a well-to-do tenant. The heriot varied from 1d to the best goods or the best beast.

The Court reported in 1792: "John Bradley dead. A life in late Smith ground and a heriot of 8/-.

do in Melcomb Yeo do Best Be(a)st & £4.

do in estate called Priors, best beast or other goods of £3-6-8.

A life in Huntleys, Heriot 5/-."

John's wife died in 1795 and the payments were repeated. The Survey of 1678 reads like this. "Henry Cornish of London. A tenement called Tynts. Three acres in East Field, three acres in West Field. Rent 6/8, Heriot £1."

The land was on a repairing lease, and in 1696 the Court states: "We continue to present against Samuel Vigor to repair his mill belonging to his estate at Bilbow." It was particularly hard when a house was destroyed by fire. In 1829, "A house, shop and premises belonging to . . . held by them under the Lord of the Manor to have been destroyed by fire, and that it be forthwith rebuilt and put in proper condition for occupation as heretofore." In this case there were six copyholders involved.

From time to time the Court would draw up a list of its customs. Like the laws of the Medes and Persians they were unchangeable. Below is a list of customs from the various manors of Mells.

"We present that the gates belonging to the Common fields at the high ways are to be set up by the Lord of the Manor."

"We present that no tenants ought to put above three sheep for an acre in the Common fields of Mells and that no tenant ought to put any sheep in the field between St Thomas and Lady Day."

"We present Col Horner to keep this Cort two times in one year according to ye old custome of ye manner. (1717)" "The tenants yt belong to the Manor of Mells yt they shall put no more cattle to feed on ye said Comons yn they can keep on their estate at winter."

Tenants of the lesser manors had their rights in the Common Field: "Ye custome is that we may lett ye cattle go out from our houses into any part of the Comon only paying a pound penny for watergrass." That was Samuels, and the Rector paid the Chief Lord £1 a year for the right of his tenants to pasture on the common lands.

"We present the customs doe beare three lives, one in possession and two in reversion, and each of them dying tenant and his wife to hold widdowed estate, and at the death of each of them being tenant there is due to the Lord the best goods without doors, and if there be none to be had without they may take the best within doors as a heriot."

"We present the tenants may take sufficient houseboot, plowboot, and fireboot or gateboot and stileboot to be employed on the same tenement without waste." (Wood allowance).

"We present that the purchaser by consent may change his estate at his will and pleasure, and surrender all the estate in the copy, except money be given by someone named in ye copy or notified before the homage."

"We present that our custom is that the Lord of this Manor cannot make any estate upon any customary hold of this Manor unless the tenant in possession surrender or give consent thereto." A note in the Rectorial Court Baron Rolls adds: "In a manner belonging to an Ecclesiastical Benefice ye Custom according to ye presentment in Court is that ye Lord of ye Manner cannot make any estate upon any customary hold of ye said Manner unless ye tenant in possession

15th Century House and Churchyard Gates, New Street   *Peter Lowry*

surrender or give consent thereto. Each tenant have a right of widowhood." It is interesting to note that when the Manor of Mells became a secular manor that the custom was so strong that the right of widowhood remained.

In 1669 the Court Baron of the Rectory presented "that Mr Geo Nevil, late lord of ye Mannr hath granted estates in reversion without ye consent or surrender of ye present tenant in possession which is contrary to ye Customs of this Mannr and which no Ld of this Mannr can legally grant nor reversion take."

An example of the way in which the rights of the tenant were upheld is when Abbot Selwood built New Street in 1490. A part of the street was built upon land belonging to the Rector. "He encroached on peices of land . . . belonging to the Church of Mells.

It would be to the advantage of both the Rector and the Abbot if the pieces of land were exchanged between them." The piece of land alloted to the Rector was "12 perches in length, lying 4ft away from the land of the Rectory of Mells, called Holy Croft to the south, and against the land belonging to the Rectory of Mells called Persons Combe in the north."[3] This intervention of the Bishop in 1492 gives the date of New Street as c1490.

[1] C H S, 2, 461
[2] J D D Keilor, Buckland Dinham, 69, 1924
[3] Collectanea 111, S R S, 31, 112, 1942

Talbot from the Horner Coat of Arms   *Tom Horner*

MISCELLANY

There is a certain amount of material from ancient documents which is of interest, prior to the dissolution of the monastery of Glastonbury, and which does not fit into a general history of Mells, and this chapter will consist of extracts from some of them.

A letter from Pope Gregory IX is of particular interest. He had appointed a commission to examine into the claim of Nicholas Clark: "Nicholas Clark has informed us that he has been prefectatus to the vacant Church of Melnes by the true patron(s) the Bishop S, a clerk of Bath diocese, the son of the last priest to officiate in that church *(qui proximo ministravit)* opposed the possession. (He had obtained possession of the Vicar's portion, and sought to keep Nicholas out of the Church.)

One of the difficulties of the medieval church was to enforce the celibacy of the clergy. At the Council of Winchester in 1076 it was ordered that all canons should put away their wives, but the parish clergy continued to marry for some considerable time. It is possible that the Rector of Mells was one of those who had a wife, or as she would have been called, a concubine. In law the eldest son inherits his father's estate. Here we have the Rector's son claiming the Vicar's portion, the rectorial stipend or part of it as his right. There was always the danger of the church losing land in this way. This was in 1230.

As much of our information comes from legal documents, it tends to be one-sided. At the same time it does give us an insight into the life of the people of other days. Money was as important then as now, and it would seem that there were those who, as today, objected to and tried to evade taxes, as well as the tax collector who tried to get taxes which were not due.

Abbot Selwood's survey of the Manor of Mells showed: "The rents of assise and customary tennantes there, apertyning unto the saide mannour, with the workes and customes, which they are bound to doe by tenure of their lands are of yearly value of £37-18-4½. Rentes and fynes. The scyte of the said mannour, with the demaynes appertynyng to the same, are letten by indenture for the somme of £6-6-8."

"Perquisites of Courtes and Fynes. The profittes of the courtes, fynes, and other casualties, are answered to the King's highness this year at £27-3-3."[1]

In addition to these was the Tithe, a tax on the annual profit of the land. In Mells this would go to the Rector. So we have the Lord of the Manor, the Pope, the King, and the Rector all expecting to get something out of the "men of Mells".

In 1450 the people of Leigh on Mendip "threatened and still daily threaten to carry away and disposed of certain fruits, and tenths and proceeds of the said Church which belong to the Rector."

There is an old rhyme which goes:

"We've cheated the parson, we'll cheat him again,

For why should the Vicar have one in ten?"[2]

Some years earlier in 1415, "the taxcollectors, that they unjustly by colour of their office, at Mellys, the close of John Tucker entered, and 4 oxen and 1 horse, with 5 marks, took and led away, the said oxen and horse detained."[3]

The collectors defended themselves declaring "that in the 8th Edward 2, (1315) the manor of Mellys was assessed at £4-6-8, and that the seneschal of the abbey of Glastonbury agreed with the collectors to pay £20 in gross . . . that Mellys was assessed at 30/- and that from the date aforesaid the men of Mellys had paid the 30/-, besides the £4-6-8." The defendant was a freeman and a free tenant of the Manor.[4]

In the time of Edward I the "Abbot of G was summoned to show by what warrant he withdrew from the King the suit of Melles due at the Sheriff's towin and 2/- of annual rent, and by what warrant he withdrew £11-18-10 from the sheriff and from the aid of the Purification without licence." The jury found in favour of the King and the Sheriff was ordered to "distrain upon the men of Melles the said 2/-," but the King "grants to Abbot of Glastonbury that they be quit of the 2/- yearly issuing out of those £11-18-10 which remained to them by an agreement between Robert of Bath and Wells and the said Abbot, which 2/- lately recovered."

If we were looking for the origin of the word Vobster we may find the answer in the following: "and an old fulling mill on the water of Melnecumbe above Fobbestor which Henry Maber once held with lands adjacent, namely, next the water of Melnecumbe ascending to the path called Hullingweye which is in the east part of the wood Seperigge and then ascending under the same path to the high road called Colier Weye, along the same road to the enclosure Ralph Fobbestor held, the land on the north of Beverbroc is called the

Breche."[5]

It is in the courts that the Horner family first appear. "Order by the officials of the Bishop of Bath and Wells to the curates of the churches of Mells, Kymmersdon, Dulting, and Babington, with regard to the proposed purgation of Robert Horner the elder, late of Mellys, but now of Dulting, charged with stealing oxen, sheep, and other animals from divers persons, especially from Richard Altofe of Babington. They are to give notice on Sunday next, at the time of divine service, that the said Richard Altofe and any other objectors to the purgation are to appear before the official in the new chapel of the cloister of the cathedral church of Wells. 1 Oct 1449."

In 1504 John Horner of Leigh appeals against the tax collector "that he by force and arms, viz, with staves, and bows and arrows ... his close and house at Leigh broke open and entered, and 9 cows, and 6 oxen, value £10, and 3 spoons of silver, a mazer, bound with silver and partly guilt ... 12 yards of woolen cloth, coloured white, four yards of woolen cloth, coloured yellow, four elnas of linen cloth of holland, half a yard of damask, 1½ yards of velvet, 4 elnas of worsted, 5 pairs brigandines, 2 salettes, 4 blades called swords, a knife, called a wood knife, a bow, a saddle and two bridles, together worth 80 marks."[6]

In 1524 "an action was brought against John Horner, of Lygh, gent, for taking possession of a messuage etc, in Mells, called Farm Place, and also certain corn, cattle, and household stuff. The council, however found that Mr Horner had, by indenture, purchased the same land."[7]

The Horners are very much in the picture now. The term "gent" is applied to them and suggests that they belong to that part of society which Trevelyan calls "for the most part ambitious squires or knights who had made money in commerce."[8] They hold land of the Abbot in Mells, Leigh, Doulting and other places. They too were employed by the Abbot as bailiffs and in other activities as when in 1476 Robert Horner with others enquired into the patronage of Nunney. In 1529 the Abbot leased to Sir Robert Horner "the manor of Haydon with premises at Haydon and Radstock."

Ten years later Wm Payne sold all his lands in Mells to Thomas Horner "including the Capital Messuage called Frenchous alias Lytyllcote Fraunces." This meant that he had purchased the lease, and held the land under the Lord of the Manor.

It is from the same sources that we get an insight into the status of women at this early period. In a matrimonial suit, in 1342, Wm

Pleytenyn, of Mells, was bound to live peaceably with his wife, and "not exceed the limits of conjugal chastisement by breaking her limbs or hurting her seriously."[9]

Deeds drawn up in respect of lands transferred from one to another give some idea of the "wealthiness" of those who so impressed Abbot Selwood. "Lease by Wm Torre of Mells, clothmaker, to Richard Chokke, knight, and one of the justices of the King's Bench; Wm Powlet, Hy Champeny, Wm Seward all Esquires, Thos Braas, John Dyker, Wm Palmer, John Vigour all gentlemen, John Torre, Sr, John Meryst, Richard Dorset, Wm Smith all Clothworkers; of his land and tenements in Mells for 20 years. Given at Mells, 12 Dec. 15 Ed IV."[10]

Sometimes rent was paid in kind. "By fine made at Ilchester in octave of Purification (27 Henry III), the Abbot of Glastonbury grants to Ernisius of Dunheved 4 messuages, 3 ferlings and 15 acres of wood and appurtenances in Mells to hold of him and his successors for ever rendering yearly 4 pounds of wax at Abbot's court of Pilton, half Easter and Michaelmas."[11]

It is seen that the Horner family had for a century been connected with Mells, and that they held land there. To end this chapter which takes us up to the dissolution of the monastery at Glastonbury we note that in 1535 "Nicholas Fitzjames, of Wolleston, gent, sold to John Horner of Michel Stoke, gent, of all the lands at Trudoxhill, Cloforde and Nuneye."[12]

[1] C H S, 2, 463
[2] S H E, IV,92
[3] S A S, XXX, 1, 57
[4] ibid
[5] S R S, Feet of Fines, 161, 77-78.1892 Ralph, however, probably took his name from the village rather than vice versa. It derives from the Anglo-Saxon personal name Fobba and Old English tor, a hill. The bounds mentioned in the conveyance, drawn up in 1233, illustrate the antiquity of local place-names. Melcombe and Shipperidge are still in use, the last named appearing in the Saxon charter of 942 as Schippeburg, a mis-rendering of Scipperugge. Breche, now spelt Breach, derives from the Anglo-Saxon word braec, land newly taken into cultivation
[6] S A S, XXX, i, pp.57-8
[7] ibid
[8] English Social History
[9] Bath & Wells, Hunt
[10] Collectanea III, ibid, 22, 110
[11] The Great Chartulary of Glastonbury, S R S, 1, 212, 1947
A ferling is a fourth part of an acre, or hide
[12] Horner MSS

THE CHURCH

The best introduction to this chapter would appear to be Leland's description of Mells shortly after the dissolution of the monastery in 1539:

"Melles standeth sumwhat clyving, and hath bene a praty Townlet of Clothing. It longgit onto Glessenbyre. Selwood Abbate of Glessenbyre seeing the Welthiness there of the People, had thought to have reedified the Townlet with mene Houses of square Stones to the Figure of an Antonie Crosse (T), whereof yn deade he made but one streatlet. The Chirche is faire and buildid yn time of mynde, ex lapide quadrato, by the hole Paroche. One Garlande, a Draper of London, gave frely to the Building of the Vestiarie, a fine and curiose Pece of Worke. One . . . Gentilman dwelling ther yn the Paroche made a fair Chapelle in the North Side of the Chirche. There is a praty Maner Place of Stone harde at ye Weste End of the Chirche. This be likelihod was partely builded by Abbate Selwoodde of Glasteinbyre Syns it servid the Fermer of the Lordship. Now Mr Horner hath boughte the Lordship of the King."[1]

Several suggestions have been made as to the origin of the name Mells. A popular one is Melles, honey, another Mills, a third one is a corruption of the word Mael,[2] Saxon for crucifix. The second derivation is certainly the right one: in medieval and early Tudor records the village is called Milnes or Melnes, analogous to the French *meaulnes*, meaning 'mills'. At one time there were some 30 small mills along the stream between Mells and Coleford.

Leland died in 1552 and the Church was built "yn time of mynde." A rough estimate is 1450. John Sammel bequeathed "to the building of the tower of Mells £3" in 1446. In 1524 John Robins left "to the Church in Mells £20 with the £7 that I gave to the making of the vestrye there." This suggests that the Church was completed in the last part of the century.

It must have taken a lot of courage for a small parish like Mells to pull down the existing church and to plan the building of an entirely new one. But it would appear that it was not a new idea to the parishioners. The Norman font suggests that there was a late Norman church, and this opinion is supported by the piece of dogtooth masonry found in the nave when the present floor was relaid. At the same time the 13th century altar stone was found at the entrance to the Horner Chapel, and a 13th century piscina also unearthed. The altar stone has been inserted into the present altar and the piscina has been inserted into the wall behind the organ. So the present church could easily be the third one to stand on the site.

The Church is much the same today as when it was built. The east window was raised in 1880 to make room for a reredos, and the sedilia placed a few inches back into the south wall of the sanctuary. Apart from this there have been no structural alterations.

During the Reformation there would have been changes made in the furnishing of the church. The stone altar would have been removed, the rood screen and gallery taken down, the side chapels would lose their altars and other furnishings, and the stained glass windows would either have been destroyed or left to be repaired with clear glass when necessary. At St John the Baptist's Church, Frome, the last stained glass window was removed in 1643 when Benjamin Avery, whose father lived in Mells, was paid 1/- for writing a certificate to Parliament to "certifie them that the painted glass in the Church window was taken down."[3] The only medieval glass left in Mells church is in the over windows of the centre window in the north aisle. From left to right the figures represent St Zita, patron saint of housemaids, St Agatha, St Mary Magdalen, and St Appollonia, patron saint of dentists.

The two side chapels appear to have been used, possibly the Horner Chapel as the Lady Chapel, and the chapel on the south side, dedicated to St Katherine. Both are mentioned in wills as late as 1503. There was also a chapel dedicated to St Anne which could have stood in the nave against one of the pillars. Most churches had a Lady Chapel and of course St Katherine was the patron saint of weavers.

The modern glass was mainly made in Mells by the Horwood brothers. It is said that the Horwoods' father was transported and that Prebendary Horner, the Rector and Squire, felt responsible for them and educated them in St Andrew's College which he founded in the Manor House. The Bursar of the College, Rev W W Blackwell, taught them the art of making stained glass. It is interesting to notice the development of their art. There is the very poor window in the Horner Chapel, and as one goes round the church the colours get stronger. The last window put in by the Horwood brothers was in 1882: the memorial window to Rev W W Blackwell on the north side of the chancel. This window is very good and compares favourably with the east window put in by Hardman in 1881.

The west window is by Hudson and it would seem that this window and the west door were restored at the same time as it was put

St Denis of Paris, carrying his head and holding a mason's T square, a copy of a mural in Mells Church. It was destroyed soon after W W Wheatley painted this picture.

in in 1851. In the upper vestry there are some fragments of medieval glass together with some of a later date from the Continent.

The restoration of the church was begun by Rev Prebendary J S H Horner. His main concern appears to have been the roofs. His son Rev George Horner said that he remembered a ceiling in the nave and that he had been told that originally the remainder of the church was the same, and that when the ceilings were removed, there was no carved woodwork.[5] The roof of the Horner Chapel must have been an exception. This is an original roof. The roof over the organ is a copy of it, the work of Wm Brown in 1846. The chancel roof was put in in 1859 through the generosity of Sir J S Hippesley. The nave roof, which is much more in keeping with the general design of the church, was erected in the same period.

In this early stage of the restoration work the raised pews of the Horners and the Rectory were made to correspond with the other pews. The elaborate memorials of the Horners and of the former rectors were removed. A description of the chancel before this reads:

"In the chancel is a handsome monument of white and Sienna marble, with an elegant and just description to the memory of the late worthy rector, Thomas Paget, S T B who died A D 1783, aged 78"[6] Another: "in the north aisle is a stately mural monument of white and grey marble in memory of Geo Horner d 1707." The two 19th century memorial brasses of the rectors Paget and Bishop, which were originally in the chancel, are against the walls of the organ chapel.

The medieval screens which enclose the two chapels were replaced with new screens which are copies of the originals with the exception of the colouring. These were made by Uriah Cooper of Trudoxhill, who also made the lectern, credence table, litany desk, and altar rails, and incorporated into them pieces from the original screens. On these can be seen some of the original colouring. The date of erection was c1855.

It was Rev George Horner, the Prebendary's son, who completed the restoration and left the interior of the church as it is today. The walls were stripped of plaster and the old Jacobean pews replaced with the present seating. This latter was planned by his father as the pew-ends were carved by the Clark brothers who had been taught to carve by Rev Edmund Stansfield in the Prebendary's time. Each pew-end is different. Some of the old pew-ends and the old panels were used to form a dado around the church, and the vestries were panelled with what remained. The chancel screen, the carving by Stillman of Bath, was erected and the present choir stalls put in. The wooden pulpit, referred to as

St Andrew's Church before Restoration 1880   *J and W Long*

Jacobean, but probably the Pulpit Set mentioned in the Churchwardens' Accounts of 1724, the work of Richard Buscombe, and costing £26-5-0, was replaced.

The present stone pulpit was installed in 1880 and carved *in situ* by G Vennell. He and his son carved the angels in the chancel and erected the altar and reredos. The chancel and the porch walls were given an ashlar facing; the latter was done by F & G Brown, of Frome. The floor of the church was tiled. The freestone floor laid in 1677 had been replaced with blue stone flags in 1814. The wrought iron candle brackets and the chandeliers in the nave, which were made up from old Bruton sconces, are the work of Singers of Frome. The gates to the chancel, the gate leading from the choir into the vestry, and the choir stall fronts were designed by H Woodyer, the architect who supervised the restoration, and are the work of Filmer and Mason of Guildford.

The stripping of the walls and the retiling of the floor must have led to the removal of many memorials of prominent persons who had lived in the parish, as well as those of the Horner Family and the Rectors

Sir Wm Nicholson window in the Parish Church   *Peter Lowry*

Memorial to Edward Horner   *photo by Tom Oates*

referred to earlier. One very beautiful memorial remains in the
chandelier (1721) which hangs in the chancel. The plaques in memory
of the Horner Family are probably taken from more elaborate

memorials taken down by Prebendary Horner. To compensate for this loss the Horners in 1872 placed the "tomb" in the Chapel bearing the coats of arms of all those who lie buried in the vault below: the work of F Nicholls of Lambeth. The Fussells erected the serpentine memorial which is set in the wall to the south of the tapestry picture designed by Burne-Jones and worked by Lady Horner. Lady Horner also worked the white Altar Frontal.

It was this lady who brought to the church and village many works of art. When her son Mark died in 1908 she had water from the Manor reservoir laid on to various points of the village as a memorial to him. At two points, Woodlands End and Little Green, the taps were placed in especially erected walls, and the inscriptions on them are the work of the sculptor Eric Gill. The lettering of the Raymond Asquith memorial under the tower is the work of the same artist and also the Mark Horner memorial stone in the churchyard. Also under the tower on the opposite wall is a memorial to Laura Lyttleton, a gesso designed by Burne-Jones. The War Memorial in the church was designed by the College of Art in Kensington. In the Horner Chapel* there is an equestrian memorial to Edward Horner, the last direct male heir to the Horner Estate, who was killed at Cambrai in 1917. The horse and rider are the work of Sir Alfred Munnings and the base was designed by Sir Edwin Lutyens. Sir Edwin also designed the village War Memorial, the Park House, when rebuilt after being destroyed by fire in 1917, the music room and loggia in the manor house, and the shelter at Woodlands End. The east window of the Horner Chapel is the work of Sir William Nicholson, who also did the wooden tablet resting on the Horner tomb and giving something of the history of Edward Horner. It is interesting to note that the sculpture is the first of only two which Munnings did and as far as is known the window by Nicholson the only one he designed. Baroness Asquith once observed to the author that Lady Horner must have been a remarkable woman to be able to persuade two such men to make a break in their traditional forms of art.

Some would say that the church has been over-restored, but it is difficult to condemn those, who, at various times in the history of the church, were faced with the problem of maintenance and restoration. In earlier days the work of repair was carried out by local craftsmen under the guidance of the Rector and Churchwardens. The restoration carried out by the Horners was by and large well done. They were influenced by the fashion of the time, which was not in the best taste, and yet one

*This statue was moved to the back of the North aisle in 2006, to create a small chapel for worshippers where it had stood.

is conscious that an attempt was made to preserve, as far as possible, the original character of the church.

During the Second World War the church had a narrow escape when a stick of dud bombs fell in the Fairground on the east side of the building; their subsequent disposal smashed some panes of glass in the church.

Col Thomas Strangways Horner, who died in 1844, was the last of the Horner family to be buried in the vault in the Horner Chapel. Since then the Horners have been buried against the eastern wall of the churchyard. Near them can be found memorials to Baroness Asquith, Ronald Knox, the Roman Catholic priest and scholar, and Siegfried Sassoon. Nearer to the east end of the church can be found the memorial of Canon Hannay, a former Rector, and better known as George A Birmingham the novelist. In the north east corner of the churchyard is a memorial to Reginald McKenna, a cabinet minister under Asquith. This memorial is the work of Sir Edwin Lutyens, as are the memorials to Sir John and Lady Horner.

In the tower there is a peal of eight bells. The original peal was five bells and these were recast into six in 1717 by Abraham Rudhall. Of these two remain, no 4, inscribed "Prosperity to the Church of England." T. Bilbee recast no 3 and the tenor in 1745, and Wm. Bilbee no 6 in 1788. Two bells were added in the 19th century. The tenor bears the inscription:

I to the Church the living call

To the grave do summon all.

There is a faceless clock. The earliest mention of it is in 1658: "George Sweet for keeping the Clock and oil for the Clock and Bells." In 1720: "Pd James Clark of ffrome for setting up the Clock and Chimes, £37-2-0," and in 1792: "Paid Mr Jones (Bath) for Altering and Repairing the Clock and Chimes, £40." The clock strikes the hour and the quarters and plays one of four tunes every three hours. The present drum replaced an older wooden drum which may have played the chimes of 1720.

[1] S A S, XXXIII, 11, 133-34
[2] S A S, XXX, 1, 64
[3] Belham, P, The Making of Frome, FSLS, 19, 1973
[4] White MS
[5] S A S, XXXIX, 21
[6] C H S, 11, 464

BUILDINGS

"Melles standeth sumwhat clyving, and hath bene a praty Townlet of Clothing."

As one enters Mells from Frome, the view from the top of Lime-kiln Hill suggests that the Mells of Leland's time did appear to be clinging to the Rock and the rising ground leading up to the church and dominated by its massive tower. The church had not long been finished and was only just beginning to weather, and the tower would stand out nearly white against the background. It was a very different Mells from the Mells of today. The existing Manor House (built by Glastonbury Abbey) had not yet been extended, nor the present Rectory. The only buildings remaining apart from the church are the Tithe Barn and the houses in New Street. The little stream running through the "Person's Combe" ran across the road at the Rectory Corner and at Woodlands End.

Abbot Selwood had seen the need for improving the housing conditions for the increasing number of wealthy people. The houses in New Street give some idea of the kind of house they expected. The first house on the right as one enters the street is a good example. It has changed little since it was erected.

Mells Manor and Church as painted by W W Wheatley in 1845. The Manor House was then in use as a farm. This is an unusual view taken from the village side.

The first great change was the extension of the Manor House in 1590 and then again in the early 18th century. The present house is the south wing only of that enlarged building which was formed as the letter H. In 1740-1760 the north wing and the connecting arm were pulled down* to form the stables of the new Park House.

It is possible that the hundred years following the building of the Manor House was one of much building activity. The cottages at Garston Gate are dated 1598. The first house on the right as one enters the street from the south was in fact two houses with a connecting arched passage through which horses were led to the forge behind. The Rectory Terrier of 1638 speaks of a tenement "in the tenure of Mr Thomas Horner containing one fair house newly builded," and another with "a Smith's forge newly builded." Other tenements too were referred to as "faire," and one as a large house "fitt for Clothing trading, all houses fitt for it, as Tucking Mill, Dyehouse, Woll Loft." In addition to these there is a cottage on the Rock with a beautiful Elizabethan fireplace, and others

Mells Park House before the fire

*Sir John Horner told a meeting of the Somersetshire Archaeological Society at Mells on May 28, 1923 that "they knew of the other wing for certain because two or three years ago, in the abnormally dry weather, the foundations of the lost wing showed up quite clear on the lawns". (Proceedings of the Bath and District Branch, 1919-1923, 186.)

Destruction of the old Mells Rectory

can be found in the Rectory Cottages. Houses built for poorer people would only have lasted for a generation or two.

The next major change came when the Horners built Mells Park House in 1740. The Park was extended and probably for the first time enclosed. The extension meant the removal of the manor mill from the Duckery to Bilboa, and the roads leading to the old mill becoming private roadways.

The building of the Rectory followed soon afterwards about 1790. This was to change the whole character of the village. The new parsonage and its land were enclosed behind a wall. Houses standing on the site were demolished, including the old Parsonage House, the original Poyntz House, and the house in which Cornish, the one time Sheriff of London, had lived. A meadow, part of which remains at the Rectory Corner, was enclosed, and the roadway which ran from Garston Gate directly into the Manor stable yard entrance, diverted to its present position. The ford across the road was tunnelled under a new road which ran along the north wall of the Rectory. It is possible that the roadway in front of the Rectory cottages was raised at this time. The Mells of Leland's time was gone for ever.

The present Poyntz House may suggest that Richard Poyntz had also decided that his house was not all that a man of his position could wish, and that he built a larger and more modern one. After all he did drive a coach and six horses, and had his own family pew.

Mells was to change very little until after the First World War. At the peak of the coal period a row of rather unsightly houses was built on the Little Green, and two rows of houses, one in Upper Vobster and one in Lower Vobster. After the war a row of Council houses was built at Longfield. The sale of a large part of the Estate in 1923 meant that the way was open for the first time for private building, but the major building has been done by the Rural District Council. The Fairview Estate followed the Second World War, and, with the Longfield Estate, has been enlarged in recent years. A slum clearance scheme after the Second World War led to the pulling down of a couple of cottages and the renovation of others. One outstanding example of preservation and renovation is that on Little Green where an old blacksmith's shop has been incorporated into the house. Other cottages have been restored and appear much as they have done for the past hundred or so years.

Mells Park House as rebuilt to the design of Lutyens in 1924   *Peter Lowry*

The upkeep of a property on a big estate has always been a problem. Under the manorial system the tenant was responsible for the repairs and the Court Rolls reveal that so often the tenants failed to fulfil their obligations. Later when the rents for cottages were 1/- or 1/6 per week the landlord could not always afford to spend much on his property. Richard White, who lived at Holwell Farm in the early part of the 19th century, wrote of Prebendary Horner that "he spent a great deal of money in improving the cottages that had got into a bad state." Lady Horner, writing nearly a century later, recorded that "the cottages of Mells were very old, very picturesque, and very unfit for modern standards of life. The roofs, generally of thatch, and miserably bad, leaked everywhere . . . they had small windows, stone floors, damp walls and steep staircases. And none of the farms were in good order.[1]"

Branch Farm where there was a house from at least the 12th century, has the remains of its 15th century predecessor. Prospect Farm has an attractive façade, and so have Bilboa and the School House. A building worthy of note is the Blind House or lock up. The Court Leet of 1728 presented "Thomas Horner and Rev Mr Paget to erect a guard house, and to put the Stocks and whipping post in Good repair as it was when taken down." A survey of Mells dated 1678 records "a tenement or messuage house and garden near the pillory."

Mells Rectory rebuilt

The present Melcombe would have been built at that time, and it suggests that the piece of "Lord's waste" in front of the Blind House[2], had been the site of these new aids to law and order for several hundred years.

Wadbury House is a fine example of solid Victorian work. It was built c1840 by the Fussells who had the Iron Works in the valley below. The Park House was burnt down and Lutyens was the designer of its successor.

The ruins of an ancient barn at Mells. It was burnt down by an incendiary on March 2, 1845 and painted by W W Wheatley soon afterwards. The Government offered £100 reward for the discovery of the culprit, as did Rev Mr Horner

[1] Time Remembered, Horner
[2] Thomas Bunn, of Frome, noted in his diary on January 7, 1845: "Mr. Fussell's newly erected mansion is a charming residence, the design for which was drawn by Mr. ——— , of Bath." The architect's name has been left blank in the original

THE HORNERS

Windham and Horner, Berkley and Thynne,
When the abbots went out, they came in.

Henry VIII had two allies in suspending the monasteries. One is seen in the growing charges of 'heresies' being made by the bishops; the reformation on the continent was having its influence on this country; and there were our own Lollards. The second ally was the growing number of rich middle class who were land hungry. The most the latter could do was to hope to hold a manor under a patron, such as the Abbot of Glastonbury, as did Sir Thomas Horner: the Manor of Haydon. It was not difficult for the king to find true and loyal men to sit on a jury and to condemn an abbot like Whiting, good man though he was. Thomas Horner in 1539 sat on the jury that sentenced the abbot to death.[1]

Once the king owned the land the next thing was to sell it. Thomas Horner bought the manors of Stanton Prior and Ashwick in 1540. John Horner, of Stoke St Michael, the Manor of Cloford in 1542, and Thomas and John the manors of Mells etc*. From *Letters and Papers Henry VIII* we get the following information: "Wells, Somerset, 1543 July 10. Thomas Horner and John Horner Junr Grant in fee to the said John for £1831-19-11¼ of the manors of Melles, Lye and Nonney Somerset, which belonged to Glastonbury monastery, the advowsons of Mells Rectory, Lye chapel, and Nonney rectory and a pension of 20s out of Mells rectory; also the farm of Luyde and lands called Luyde in Yevell Parish; which belonged to Glastonbury, in tenure of Lady Eliz Fitz James, widow; also the manor of Discowe alias Discove, Somerset which belonged to Brewton monastery, with appertenances in Discowe and Holy Waters alias Holy Fathers; and lands in Battecombe, which belonged to Taunton Priory."[2]

By 1554 lands held by the family included "manors and lands at Trolockeshyll, Doulting, Holcombe, Prydy, Westharter, Eastharter, Sammford, Wynscombe, Churchyll, Pukston, Weake and Yatton."
The Horners already held a good deal of land in Mells and in the neighbourhood. These properties were leaseholds; the Horners now become landowners.

As far as Mells is concerned it was John Horner, of Cloford, who established the family home there. Thomas was a bachelor. In addition to the lands already mentioned, Thomas had bought the manors of Eodden and Flintford, and Brampsters Farm in Mells.

*Horner bought Cloford Manor from Roger Bassing of Cirencester

Cloford Manor   *A R Yeates*

John Horner, of Cloford, had a son who married Meriel, daughter of John Malte, "citizen and merchant tailor of London." He also was the King's Sergeant. "It was John Malte who designed, made and fitted the clothes of Henry VIII with which Holbein has made us familiar."[3]

Thomas Horner gave the young couple the manors of Flintford and Rodden, and John Malte the manors of Doulting and Milton Puddimore with the hamlet of Stoke St. Michael. In addition to this the bachelor uncle left young John the Manor of Mells when he died. Young John was now a considerable landowner.

It is not surprising that he wanted to follow the example of other great landowners, like the Thynnes of Longleat, and build himself one of the new and magnificent houses for which the period is famous. This house he built at Mells. It was built in the shape of the letter H and is said that "among all the houses of the period in which the neighbourhood is so rich, the Manor House was the most important with the single exception of Longleat."[4]

One has a suspicion that the rhyme of Little Jack Horner, so long associated with the family, was applied to them at this time. It implies that the Horners did not buy the Manor of Mells, but stole it. This satire on a successful family says that Thomas Horner, entrusted with the surrendered deeds of Glastonbury Abbey, on his way to London to deliver them to Cromwell, took for himself the deeds of Mells from the pie in which they were hidden. The plum was the Manor, however the Manor House at Mells existed before the dissolution of the monasteries. John Horner the younger started to extend it but it was his son, the second John Horner (1546-1612) who made it into an H-shaped House.

We find no member of the family became a national figure. The Horners were Lords of the Manor and as such took their place in the local affairs of their neighbourhood and county. They represented the county in Parliament as Knights of the Shire, they were Lieutenants of the County of Somerset and the City of Bristol; sheriffs of the counties of Gloucester and Somerset; and colonels of the Militia and of the Frome Volunteers, later to become the North Somerset Yeomanry.

Several members of the family were knighted, which suggests that their services were appreciated in higher quarters. The last to be knighted was Sir John Horner, who in 1895 was appointed the Commissioner of Woods and Forests by Lord Rosebery. On his retirement in 1907 he was created a K C V O by Edward VII.

Their close link with the neighbourhood is seen in their marriages. They married into the Speke family of Whitelackington, the Fortesques of Devonshire, the Pagets of Cranmore, the Ilchesters, the Strangways of Dorset, and Hippesleys of Ston Easton, and later they went further afield and married into the Stuart family, and through their Scottish connections, the Graham family. It was through this last marriage that the family linked up with the Asquiths. Sir John and Lady Horner moved in political circles and many of the leading Liberals were entertained at Mells. Katharine Horner married Raymond Asquith, son of the Prime Minister, who on his retirement became the first Earl of Oxford and Asquith. The last male heir, Edward Horner having died, Mrs Raymond Asquith inherited the manor after the death of her mother, Lady Horner. Her son Julian succeeded to the title.

The only Horner to serve in the forces overseas was Edward who was killed at Cambrai in 1917. But Sir John Horner fought on the side of Cromwell, and until he was taken prisoner in Bristol by Prince Rupert, played an active part in the campaign. A B the gossip writer said that: "Sir John was discharged upon his Parole of Honour not to act any more against the King, which he faithfully observed and lived retired to the King's death."

Oldmixon says "that in 1642 Sir John Horner commanded the Somerset Militia and armed his servants and retainers. His memory and merits do honour his name. He wished to drive the Array men, under Lord Hertford out of Wells. He marched from Chewton Mendip, and lay all night in the hills, had a furze bush for a bed and said it was the best bed he ever lay on. However no collision took place between his party and the Royalists." Sir John appears to have been of the force which entered Wells in 1642. It was on this occasion that "they broke the painted windows in the cathedral, and made havoc with the wine, organs and pictures in the palace; one picture, which was thought to represent the Blessed Virgin, being carried about and mocked."[5]

King Charles visited Mells on 17 July 1644. "The king lay at Sir John Horner's house at Mells, a faire large house of stone, very strong, in the form of an H; two courts. . . The Church is very large and faire adjoining. Horner is in rebellion, his estates sequestrated £1000 per annum."[6] The King's retainers stayed at Kilmersdon. It was from Mells that the King sent his letter to the city of Wells asking for a loan of £500 to be repaid "when God enabled him to do it."[7]

The Rector of Mells had thrown in his lot with the King, and Sir John had appointed the Rev Richard Fairclough in his stead, a priest with Presbyterian sympathies. In 1647, a plan for settling the Presbyterian government of Somerset was prepared by John Horner and five others. A B writes: "As the self-denying Ordinance had changed the complexion of the Party, and the Independents had flung the Presbyterians out of their plan, and were resolved not to restore, but entirely overthrow the ancient Constitution of their kingdom, Sir John, like many other worthy gentlemen, had time to reflect upon their past proceedings, and bewail the calamities they had concurred upon their Country. These must be his sentiments, for when the news of the King's murder was brought to Mells, and the Ringers set about ringing the bells, Sir John, old as he was, took a good oaken stick in his hand, and played it so well in the Belfry that he stopped their music and rejoicing."

Sir John died in 1659 and was buried at Mells. A remarkable man with an original wife. In her will she asked that "£100 to be expended about my funeral, no part to be laid out in Blackes for mourning, but in buying rings for my relations and children."

Hutchins in his History of Dorset states that "when the King's affairs declined, Sir John I presume regained possession, and the attainder was forgotten perhaps, and dying before the Restoration, certainly not enforced." What is certain is that Sir John's son George inherited the estates and was knighted by Charles II.

It is here that we come to the only bit of scandal in the long history of the family. George's son Neville, A B tells us, was "highly hated and abhord, and very deservedly so if half what was said of him was true. His murdering Mr Winter by running his sword into his back as he was opening a gate on their way to Lansdown Hill to fight a duel, must prove him, if the story is true, a complete scoundrel. It is certain he was forced to flee into Holland . . . and probably returned in King William's time, or rather came over with him when so many fugitives and outlaws were restored to this country." He was an embarrassment to the family and his father had to provide for him. He lived at Doulting.

Although Sir George was buried at Cloford, it is during his time that the family really took root in Mells. In the Churchwardens' records of that period we find that Sir George Horner bought seats on the north side of the Church which were "laid to Samuels farm, Frenchouse and Normans." One seat was bought "for the lodj house." At this time seats were leased to householders for life, and Sir George bought a number in the north aisle, and these must have formed the original family pew. Seats became free c1880.

In troubled times the leading figures in local affairs could become suspect. In 1716 there was a Jacobite rising in the north and a round-up of suspected sympathisers took place in the south-west. A B writes: "That in the year 1716 when Colonel Halse apprehended Sir Wm Windham, a captain and a party of soldiers came to Mells to seize Colonel Horner; that owing to an intelligence sent to him by Mr Phelps of Frome he just escaped them and got to a Farm house a little way from his own; that when the captain came to the door he asked Mr Read where his master was. "Not at home" says Read. "You lie" says the captain.

Guard set on all sides, the house searched, rummaged and ransacked; that when the Colonel's Commission was found from the Duke of Ormond it was concluded that he was a Jacobite and a traitor, and the more pains taken to find him out; that he disguised himself as a

Farmer or Drover driving cattle to Smithfield: that the first place that he appeared as himself was in the House of Commons; that he had no more trouble given him." Of the Colonel's wife A B wrote: "A most engaging woman, a false wife, and a monster of hypocracy and dissimulation."

Colonel Thomas Strangways Horner (1688-1741) built Park House. There is a contract in the Horner archives dated 27 November 1724, between T S Horner and Nathaniel Ireson of Stourton; Ireson agrees to build Horner a house in the park for £210 in 1725.

The Rectory, a former clothiers house, was made over to Rev T Paget by Thomas Horner in 1762, but returned to the Horners by the mid 19th century.

In the records of the Horner family, by Sir Herbert Jekyll, it states that "the house as originally designed, was certainly completed before the middle of the 18th century, and had at that time become the family residence. The Manor House was no longer occupied, at the latest, after 1747, and was allowed to fall into decay. It had been considered unhealthy, perhaps not without reason, and it will be recalled that three of the children of George Horner (1646-1708) had died there. The abandonment of the Manor House may have been due partly to the change of fashion. Tudor Houses were little thought of in the 18th century, and were indeed almost regarded as barbarous. While the new house was building, the park was enlarged and many trees planted. . . Some of the oak trees, which are of great age, must have been in existence before the Park was enclosed."

Of George Horner, A B writes: "In the time of this gentleman great improvements were made in the lands of the Parish of Mells. About the year 1678 there was hardly a hedge between the Churchyards of Mells and Babington. When first the tenants made application to their Lord for leave to enclose their lands, they were refused, and the reason given was this: 'It will spoil my son's hunting.' The Park was also much enlarged, the eastern part being taken into the same, where the Grove of Beech is now. About 1690 the same was a field of oats." A B is obviously referring to the general enclosures which appear to have taken place about 1720. In the *Gentleman's Magazine*, 1794, it says that "Half the old house is mouldering in ruins, the rest is occupied by a farmer."

Col Thomas Strangways Horner "completed the additions to the Park, which his Father began. His main contribution was the West Wing including the Library designed by Sir John Soane. The dilapidated part of the Manor was finally demolished, and the stone was used in building the addition to the Park House. At about the same time the lakes were formed, and the Park assumed much of the aspect which it bears today."[1] There is one big difference however now, "the Grove of Beech," mentioned above, was cut down in recent years as the trees had become diseased.

The Horner family now enters that period of country life of which Trevelyan wrote: "The poor suffered by the War. But at no period had the landed gentry been wealthier or happier or more engrossed in the life of their country houses."

"Central peace subsisting at the heart

Of endless agitation."[9]

Lady Horner in her *Time Remembered* wrote of her arrival in Mells as a young bride in 1883, "Mells village was extraordinarily feudal, and when I first went there had an out-of-the-world atmosphere which changed very much after the war, but impressed me then, coming from the north with its more independent, hardier, strain of villagers."

An impression of life in Mells at the beginning of the 19th century comes from the memoirs of Richard White whose father farmed at Holwell Farm. He wrote: "In those days the squire had great power and knew how to use it. As he was Colonel of the North Somerset Cavalry every tenant had to join the force. I have heard my father speak of many occasions when his company or troop had to take part in quelling riots. . ." One such riot was reported in *The Globe,* Jan 26 1813: "A serious riot took place at Frome ... a drunken set of colliers endeavouring to obstruct the Peace Officers from doing their duty. . . The Frome Cavalry and infantry were called out who succeeded in securing the ringleaders who were strongly escorted to Ilchester gaol. Mr Jolliffe received a violent blow which cut through his hat; Mr Ircland, Lord Cork, and Col Horner received similar blows." Richard White goes on: "Colonel Horner was an out and out Tory. When the election came there was no canvassing of the farmers as it was understood they had to vote with their landlord. Woe to him who dared to vote to the contrary, it meant their notice to quit. As the polling was at Wells, Colonel Horner, with his tenants riding behind him, went down in a body and voted. Colonel Horner, as the Squire, also ruled the Church. At the rent audits he was in the habit of saying how pleased he was in having a son to take charge of their money, and another to take charge of their souls.

"I well remember the old gentleman in Church. He had a pew of good size, nicely carpeted, easy comfortable movable couches, with a fireplace in which there was always a good fire when the family was at church on the Sunday, in cold weather. After giving the fire a poke ... he would lean his arms on the front of the pew, with the colour of his face as red as the rose he often wore, taking stock of who was in church, when we were all shivering with the cold. When the service was over many of the Parishioners used to wait in the churchyard, making a row either side of the path, till the Colonel and his family passed by, when the men did their humble obeisance by holding the brims of their hats, and the women theirs by respectfully dropping their courtesy."

Richard White also gives a description of the Colonel's funeral in 1844 which is well worth recording: "The Colonel had a grand funeral. When the hearse with four horses got as far as the gates of Babington House, carriages with the mourners and friends and the mounted tenantry fell in behind it. The under-bearers took their places; each side of the hearse two mutes ... walked by the side of the horses, whose duty it was very frequently to turn and make a bow to the hearse and the contents. The horses had high plumes on their heads and black velvet trappings on their backs. The top of the hearse had many similar plumes. The tenantry wore long black cloaks with long black scarves hanging from their hats, and so did the bearers and others, making altogether a solemn and imposing procession. The burial took place under the church floor in the family vault."

Although the feudal atmosphere was to continue for another century, it can be said that the beginning of its decline began with the death of this Colonel Horner. That it lasted down into the thirties of the 20th century was largely due to the long lives of Prebendary Horner's children, the last of whom died in 1951. The Prebendary became a Tractarian and was probably influenced by the Christian Socialist Movement. When he became Rector in 1836 he removed the elaborate memorials of his family and of former rectors from the church; he lowered the family and the rector's pews to the same level as that of the others. He repaired the cottages which were in a bad state. He established the village school, and supported other schools in the village for the education of the middle classes. His great experiment was the establishment of St Andrew's College in the Manor House for the training of missionaries and school teachers. He began the restoration work of the five churches in his gift, and it was in his time that St Edmund's, Vobster, was built.

In Prebendary Horner there was a mixture of the new and the old. It is only natural that the old died slowly and was to rear its head again for a time. George Horner, who succeeded his father as Rector, is described by Lady Horner, in *Time Remembered,* as living with his mother and four sisters in the Rectory, and ruling over them with all the authority of church and family combined. And this authority continued in the village even to giving the village children their names. One wonders whether this was an old custom, for it is difficult to imagine where such a name as Sardinius Salmon came from if it did not come from the Manor or the Rectory. It was the Misses Horner who found the girls jobs as they left school. Some were sent to Miss Fussell's School at Chantry, where they began their training as maids with no wages at all. Poaching for the boys, and getting 'in trouble' for the girls, meant the banishment of the offender or the offender's family from the parish.

This austere Rector was a Liberal as was his son Sir John of whom Lady Horner wrote: "He was a Liberal in his political beliefs, but only out of extreme conservatism." It is recorded in the minutes of The Frome and District Clerical Society for 1883 that the Rector in response to a remark that the Co-operative Movement would extirpate the shopkeeper said: "Why should he not be extirpated? The principle of the co-operative store is good; it keeps down dishonest profits and bad debts". Lady Horner also adds "to his credit he spent his entire patrimony on the restoration of Mells Church." The First World War was to see the beginning of the final breakdown of the feudal atmosphere. Other changes were taking place. The Horner family returned to the Manor House in 1900. Lady Horner in her book says that this was for economic reasons, and that they hoped that they might be able to return to the Park House later.

The First World War came, followed by an economic depression. In 1923 there was the sale of a large part of the Estate for a fraction of its true value.* The Park House was burnt down in 1917. At that time it was let to G T Bates. It was rebuilt in 1924 by Reginald McKenna, who bought the land in 1938, selling the Park and House to a timber merchant who in turn sold it to Capt F L Trotter. With the sale of so

*4,300 acres were to be sold including numerous cottages and 22 farms. The land was spread over the parishes of Mells, Whatley, Leigh, and Cloford. A few of the lots were withdrawn at the last moment.

much land, now valuable again owing to the demand for limestone for road making, it was left to others to make their fortunes from it. The selling of several of the farms and cottages narrowed the sphere of influence of the family. Neither the Park nor the Manor owned the village, and men were free, say to keep a dog, and there was no one to deny them their right.

Yet the parish owed a great deal to the Lord of the Manor. Almost by right the village expected, and the Lord of the Manor expected too, that he should take a lead in all parish affairs. Under the manorial system he was there to order their affairs. The Lord of the Manor accepted his responsibility.

One of the first things the Horners did after they came into the Manor was to give the land, and no doubt a house, as an almshouse and school. When the present almshouses were built their donation was a very generous one. When the Workhouse came to the parish it was they who provided the house free of rent. When the reservoir at Conduit was built, it supplied not only the Manor and the Rectory, but also much of the village. There were taps in Gay Street and near the Talbot Inn. Later there were two more added in memory of Mark Horner at Woodlands End and at Little Green. It would appear that the restoration of the five churches in their gift, including Mells and Leigh, was mainly at their own expense. The last two bells of the peal of eight were gifts of the family, and so is the silver gilt Communion Set which is now priceless. The Schoolhouse is leased free to the National Society for as long as it is used for education purposes.

A school for boys was built in New Street and returned to the estate when it ceased to be used as such. A Social Club used the premises in New Street and later in the Doctor's Walk rent free. At Vobster, the Club Room was built for the use of miners and later given to the village by Lady Horner. When the Burial Act of 1880 was passed, and it was necessary to enlarge the churchyard, the necessary land was given, and in 1914 a further gift of land was made. A wheelwright's shed on the Little Green was converted into a suitable meeting place and placed at the disposal of the Women's Institute. In the centre of the village there is the Recreation Ground which is leased to the Parish at a nominal rent. The Lord of the Manor can be said to have been a benevolent autocrat.

Lady Horner says that in her early days the villagers had not yet begun to question the Divine Right of the Squire. A letter in the Rectory from a young man, Walter A Chamberlain, who ran away to Canada suggests that she was not correct. An attempt was made to get him to return, but he wrote: "I shall come to you when I am able, but to come to be a white slave, never never never."

[1] Jekyll
[2] S & D N & Q, 9, 72
[3] Jekyll, ibid
[4] Jekyll, ibid
[5] Bath & Wells, Wm Hunt
[6] S A S XXX, 1, 56
[7] Jekyll, ibid
[8] Jekyll, ibid
[9] S H E, IV 18-19

Mells Green c1900

THE RECTORS

For centuries, until recent years, every parish had its Parson or Person. The Rectory of Mells included Leigh-on-Mendip. It was a Rectorial Manor, and that there was enough land belonging to it to bring in from rents and dues about £1000 p a, in 1850. In the early days the parson was usually a farmer as well. This continued for some time after the Reformation. We find that Dr William Hill, Rector 1591-1619, not only farmed the Glebe but also bought and farmed Poolhouse Farm, Mells. Indeed he appears to have been quite a landowner. At his death he willed his lands at Filton to his son Phillipe, and his lands at Congresbury to his daughter Marye. To his daughters Prudence and Annah, he left his lands at Poolhouse which he had bought from William Sherman. He also had leases of land from the Parson of Babington as well as land at Luckington. To his wife he left "sixe of my best kyne, and all the come as shall be growinge upon her own tenementes which I now holde in her righte, at the time of my decease, and also my black mare."[1]

Near the font in Mells Church there is an incomplete list of rectors no doubt compiled from the Bishops' Registers published by the Somerset Record Society and from which most of the information in this chapter comes. There is on record that Godfry Gifford was presented with the living in 1266. His name does not appear in the list in the church, nor does that of Thomas White, whose name appears in

St Andrews Church

1554. One assumes that after the gift of the Manor to the Abbot of Glastonbury, or even before, there was a rector. William I founded the manorial system more or less as it was to continue, and Domesday suggests that by 1086 there was a fairly ordered society with the parochial system.

The origin of the Rectorial Manor must remain a mystery. It is possible that the Abbot gave the Rector a lesser manor, rather like Samuels, as an endowment for the living. Samuels had been in existence in 1226, when it passed from John Doggetail to the Samuels. Reginald, Bishop of Bath (1174-1192) grants "to the Abbot and Convent of Glastonbury for ever, that they may without any difficulty, diminus or contradictus take yearly from the Church of Mells 20/- ad opus (for the works) of the church of Glastonbury under name of pension." (yearly grant).[2] In 1292 the living was worth 15 marks.[3]

Whatever the value of the living it would appear that some of the rectors found it difficult to manage on their means or were bad managers. The King in 1309 sent to the Bishop a complaint against the Rector of Mells and other defaulters. In the answer it was stated that "all the goods sequestrated were offered for sale; they did not realise the sum required, save 5/4 at Burnet, which we are ready to pay."

From Mells the Bishop wrote a letter to the King as follows: "By Him through whom all kings do reign etc, Robert Maundeville, Clerk, (et pro Clerico habitcus) having been imprisoned for money debt in

'The old Manor House' at Leigh-on-Mendip stood behind the church; it was the home of a junior branch of the Horner family. The house was built in 1592 and was about to be demolished when painted by W W Wheatley in 1845.

18th Century Communion Set by Paul Lamarie   *Peter Lowry*

Newgate, London, contrary to Statute, (viz that clerks should not be seized as laymen, for this kind of debt) we beseech your highness for his liberation. Melles. Dec 6."[4]

Later the king is writing to the Bishop about Richard de Leighreburgh, alias Ostage, the Rector, "to raise 106s 4d on the Rectory of Mells, held by Richard le Ostage, sequestrated by our command at suit of Edmund de Morle." (A former Rector).

Andrew Sprengehuse went from Mells to the Rectory of Wrington. He was condemned: "in a certain sum of money to be paid to Master de Leith, (the new Rector of Mells) at certain terms now passed, and has not taken care to pay, thereby incurring the pain of excommunication. We command you that you study to do justice on behalf of the said John. 1332. Bishop John to John Martel his official."[5]

It is unfortunate that we know more about the defaulters than we do about those who have been loyal and devoted parish priests. The odd reference here and there gives us an insight into their way of life; that Edmund de Morle was appointed Rector before he was ordained or that "Lord Monthermer, on pilgrimage to St Iago, granted leave to Richard, Rector of Mells, to remain one year in Lord M's service, with provisoes."

That Geoffrey was the parish chaplain of Mells during Richard's absence, and "licenced to celebrate mass every Sunday, till the Feast of

St Michael, early in the morning at Legh, and high mass on the same Sundays in the Church of Mells."[6] That John de Leech, Rector, exchanged the living with Sir Robert de Helpiston, canon of Chichester and Prebendary of Waltham. Priests at this time were given the title of master and sir, and nuns the title of lady. Thus we find on May 9 1472: "Institution of Master Robert Wilson, bachelor in both laws, to the church of Mells, vacant by the death of Sir Henry Mudford, on the presentation of the Abbot and convent of Glastonbury."[7]

In 1500, Master Ralph Colynwoode was instituted by the rectory 'in the person of Thomas Scotte his proctor.' Ralph was a professor of Divinity. John de Langebergh was licenced to "reside in the cathedral church of Salisbury till Michaelmas." The Bishop "dispensed with Robert, Rector of Mells, till Christmas. That he can stay with Thomas de Heyham, his kinsman, till the feast of St Peter ad Vincula." It being a Rectorial Manor, Mells was always considered a good living, a plum. Before the Reformation, one Rector, Robert Wilson, was the Chancellor of Wells Cathedral, and Wm Baker, a Canon Residentiary.

Up to this time the appointments had been made by "the Abbot and convent of Glastonbury," or, in the case of a vacancy there, by the Bishop. On Jan 9 1556 the register records: "Institution by the Vicar General of Master George Carow, clerk, to the church of Mells on the presentation of Master John Horner of Clotforde, Esq"[8] Henry Morgan is mentioned as the Rector in 1537, two years before the dissolution of the monastery. Perhaps he is one of those referred to by Trevelyan when he wrote: "The monks suffered personally much less than used to be supposed until recent research revealed the facts. They were given adequate pensions, which were really paid. Many of them found employment, particularly as beneficed clergymen, and some as bishops. Under successive Catholic and Protestant regimes of Henry, Edward, Mary and Elizabeth, the Church was served by former monks and friars, who appear to have been able, as the rest of the clerical body, to adapt their views to the frequent changes of the time."[9] Perhaps Henry Morgan was one who remained at his post in spite of the changing times.

The Reformation was to bring about many changes. The clergy were once more to be allowed to marry. Many of the rich vestments and ornaments were removed from the church. When the present church was built many valuable gifts were given to it. As one might expect, the wealthy clothiers gave the vestments. In 1431 John Hertypole left in his will "to the high altar of Melles, one cope." Wm Byconl, a former Rector, left "my small pyx for the sacrament of the altar." Walter Payne, "one pair of vestments to celebrate on Sundays, 66/8." John Diker left "to the altar of the Blessed Mary, one gold ring. To the altar of St Catherine . . .one pair of sacramental vestments and one silver chalice." These items can only be a small part of the rich vestments and vessels which would have belonged to the church at that time. A simpler way of worship had no need for all these objects, and, sad as the loss is, it was inevitable. The desire to give the best for the worship of God however was not dead. In 1748 Mrs Strangways Horner gave the church a silver gilt Communion set: Chalice, two patens, and a flagon which bears the stamp P.L., Paul Lamerie. In 1855 the Marchioness of Bath gave a silver gilt alms dish.

The great change which was to make itself felt over the years was the rising status of the clergy in the social scale. We have seen that Dr Wm Hill was still a farmer, as would most of his predecessors have been, but he was also one of the landed gentry. Dr Hill had at least ten children, of whom seven seemed to have survived, and he lived in his "fair parsonage house" with its six lodging rooms. So indeed did his successors until Dr Paget.

We know enough about the rectors of Mells from this time onwards to be able to say that they mostly came from the families, who, like the Horners, were the new landowners. Jacob Bisse belonged to the well known family of clothiers of Croscombe. Either he or some of his family were rectors of Batcombe where their memorials can be seen. Jacob became a canon residentiary of Wells, where he was much followed for his fluent and eloquent preaching, and was a noted preacher in London. A Bisse was the rector of Batcombe at the time of the Reformation and his family bought the advowson there. Dr Hill married as a second wife, Edith Bisse, his predecessor's daughter.

A romantic figure is Henry Anketell, who became the Rector in 1620, and held the living, with several others, remaining there until about 1640. Unlike his patron, Sir John Horner, he was a royalist. A B wrote of him: "The three parishes of Mells, Hemington and Beckington, were the first of the nation that petitioned the Parliament to remove their ministers on account of their insufficiency; tho' it is notorious that two of them, namely Henry Anketell, D D, Rector of Mells, and Alexander Huish, B D, Rector of Beckington, were eminently learned; on their suspension or removal from their livings they retired to Oxford, where the King was then, and were graciously received. Huish was afterwards concerned with Brian Walton in publishing the Polyglot Bible greatly esteemed among foreign nations."

Anketell was at University College Oxford, and became a Fellow of Wadham in 1613. "He was a great royalist and was styled 'Colonel

Anketell the Priest and Malignant Doctor', for he was a soldier as well as a priest. The king thought so much of his military ability that he made him governor of Corfe Castle to defend the stronghold from the besieging forces of the Cromwellians. This he did with great gallantry, and the siege is said to have lasted 48 days. The castle surrendered at eight in the morning of February 29, 1646, and the defenders were allowed to march out with their arms and their freedom."[10] He is said to have died of wounds as a prisoner of war.[11]

The departure of Dr Anketell left Sir John Horner free to appoint a man after his own heart. He selected Richard Fairclough, a priest with Presbyterian sympathies. His tomb, which is in Banfield Fields, London, tells that he was the son of "Reverend Divine Mr Samuel Fairclough of Suffolk"; that like his father he was "eminent for his natural Parts, acquiring learning, and enfused Grace; Indued with a most piercing judgement, rich Fancy, and clear Expression, and therefore a good Expositor, a rare Orator, and excellent Preacher. His Spirit was most kind and obliging, most Publick and Generous; Chearful yet Watchful; Zealous yet Prudent; A pleasant companion, and a most faithful Friend, and pious Guide and Instructor by Doctrine and Example."[12]

From other sources we find him described as "a burning and shining light". As a preacher he was much sought after and his advice was frequently sought by people of eminent rank. Besides his usual exercises on the Lord's Day, of praying, reading the Scriptures, preaching, catechising, and administering the sacraments, he usually delivered in public an expository lecture upon the Scriptures in course, early in the morning, five days in the week, and always a considerable congregation. For many years together he used to be at his devotions and studies by three o'clock in the morning."[13]

After the Restoration of the monarchy Fairclough was unable to accept the Act of Uniformity and became a Non-Conformist. There is little doubt that he played a part in helping Sir John Horner to prepare his plan for Presbyterian government in the county. From Mells he went to London and later to Bristol. There is a small volume consisting of fourteen farewell sermons to the people of Mells. An extract of one reads: "And now farewell sacraments and Sabbaths; farewell exhortations and catechise; farewell this home and farewell this seat for ever, and within a little while farewell your discoveries and your fates. Farewell my pleasant habitation in this sweet aire of Mells. Farewell friend and foe; farewell all and the God of Glory give us Himself Who is all in all."[14]

Thanks to the gossip A B we have knowledge of some of the Rectors following the Restoration. He wrote: "Some time after the Restoration Sir George presented Henry Dutton, D D to the living of Mells. He had been Fellow of Corpus Christi College in Oxford; and had been ousted by the Godly Visitors of the University. He succeeded his wife's father, Douglas Dugdale, remarkable for his sufferings in those bad times, to the living of Evercreech in the year 1668. He became Prebendary of Whitelackington in the Church of Wells on the death of the very learned Mr Alexander Huish of Beckington, and soon after Canon of the same Church. In the account of him which is now before me, he is said to be a very good scholar, and an admirable preacher, so as to acquire the name of the Silver Tongued Dutton; and one of the most accomplished Persons of the Age for the agreeableness of his humour and conversation. He lived to be Rector of Mells for near forty years, and was succeeded by Mr Waldron, a gentleman, as I have been informed of good family in Devonshire."

From A B it is gathered that the Presbyterian influence was slow to die in Mells. He relates that: "It had been the custom of many years standing in the Parish, that upon a vacancy in that Church, several clergymen were invited to give a sermon to the Parishioners, that they might judge of the voice and abilities of their Pastor, and the Patron might have the approbation of the Parishioners in the choice. This, no doubt, was very laudable, and prevailed very probably to comply with the Puritan Humour of late times; and the opinion of that sect in relationship to Churchmanship, or the Covenant between Pastor and People."

The Vox Populi went a great way in these matters, and the patron if ever so puritanically inclined, was obliged to comply with the Humours. A certain clergyman mounted the pulpit at Mells in the time of Sir John Horner, but most unluckily began his prayer before the sermon with the Collect: Prevent us, O Lord. On which Sir John, loud enough to be heard by those who were near him said, 'I will prevent thy going there again.' The custom had continued on the death of Doctor Dutton in the Parish of Mells; an unlucky droll wag turned the custom into such strong, striking ridicule, comparing the preachers to Prize Fighters, Merry Andrews, and Mountebanks, that it was not repeated after Mr Waldron was made Rector.

"About the year 1694 Mr Gannet was made Vicar of Cloford and a few years after removed to Puddimore, by his very worthy Patron, George Horner, and brought back to Mells, where he had been curate before, by Col Thomas Horner in 1718. The late Mr Gannet who came to be curate of Mells in the declining days of Dr Dutton informed me, that at first he was very much in favour with the Parishioners, but having, after some time, preached a sermon in favour of episcopacy, the old Major cried out in the hearing of many, perhaps in the churchyard, 'the little parson brought us all to Church, and now drives us all out again'." The Major was Samuel Horner, who lived at Bilboa, or Bilbow, as it was then, and died in 1705 at the age of 87 years. "This old gentleman retained to the last his prejudice in favour of the puritans."

In his Social History of England, Trevelyan wrote: "In the early days of George III, the parson was rising in the social scale, living on equal terms with the gentry as never before."[15] When Dr Thomas Paget, (1751-1782), a connection of the Horner family, came to Mells, the old Parsonage does not appear to have been good enough for him and he moved into a house which stood very near the site of the present Rectory. His successor Dr Bishop, who married a Miss Paget, proceeded to build the present Rectory. Rev J Skinner, Rector of Camerton, wrote in his diary in 1831 when Rev J F Doveton was Rector: "Having breakfasted, I walked round his beautiful domain, nearly a mile in extent, of shrubberies and plantations. There is not such a rectory in the county; it used to be called a bishopric when the late incumbent, Dr Bishop lived there."

It must indeed have been a magnificent domain in its original state. Before being burned down in 1929, on All Fools' Day, the house had a third storey with dormer windows. The gardens were beautifully kept down to the beginning of the Second World War, and in the Summer months the parishioners were invited to walk through the grounds on Sunday evenings after Evensong. In the Diocesan maps the Glebe field is still proudly called the Park.

Rev J F Doveton, mentioned above, appears in some memoirs of one Edwin Long, a former parishioner. His father had told him about Mr Doveton: "A tall proud gentleman. He married one of his two daughters to Squire Paget of Cranmore where father did the painting, tyling and plastering as we do today. He married the other daughter to Squire Adams, of Charlton, which I think father said was out Kilmersdon way. When it was fine the Rector used to walk from the Rectory in a black silk gown and a college cap, when he was going to preach, which was always in the morning when the Colonel was at home." The only other thing I know about Mr Doveton is that he was something of an artist. My authority for this is a letter I received from someone who has a painting by him.

Of the two Horners who were rectors something has been said in the chapters on the Horner family. Rev George Horner was followed by Rev Edward Denison Lear. The son of an archdeacon of the Salisbury diocese, Mr Lear came like a breath of fresh air into the parish, and must have shocked the Misses Horner as much as did the arrival of Lady Horner.

Coming as he did immediately after Rev George Horner, who was "anti-everything" the parish must have wondered what had hit it. It was Mr Lear who put a wooden floor in the Tithe Barn and erected a stage. There were socials and dances. There were plays and pageants. Many of the older people in Mells today have been some character from Shakespeare. Many of the events took place on the Rectory lawn.

Mr Lear would be seen with his two retrievers on his way to one of the farms for a bit of ratting. He could speak to the parishioners in their own language. In all this he was aided and abetted by his wife, who was also an artist. I have often wondered why this rector's name does not appear in Lady Horner's *Time Remembered.* Perhaps the story told by the late Dr Helps may have some bearing on it; it is that he was working in his garden at Bilboa when he heard Sir John coming along the Doctor's Walk repeating aloud, "Damn that fellow Lear." A similar remark appears in one of George Birmingham's novels, *Laura's Bishop* and the doctor's story was probably the source.

Canon Hannay followed Rev E D Lear. He is known by a wider public as George A Birmingham. It would appear he found it expedient to leave Ireland after the publication of one of his literary efforts. It was before the establishment of the Republic of Eire. Rev Norman Higgins was the next Rector and he became the Archdeacon of Wells in 1940 and a Canon Residentiary in 1944.

[1] Lea Register Soame, 99
[2] Notes, G Horner
[3] C H S, ii, 464
[4] Drokensford's Register, S R S, 82, 1887
[5] Registum Radulphi de Salopia, S R S, Vol 9, 445, 106, 1896
[6] ibid, Vol 10, 2560, 662
[7] Registers of Bishop Stillington and Fox, S R S, 544, 92, 1937
[8] Bishops' Registers, 1518-1559, S R S, 857, 147, 1940
[9] S H E, Vol 1, 210
[10] Hutchins, History of Dorset
[11] Underdown, Somerset in Civil War, 144
[12] S & D N & Q, Vol 13, 133
[13] Mells Church F H, 25
[14] ibid
[15] S H E, Vol 3, 116

INDUSTRIES

William the Conqueror found England mainly an agricultural land. Mells had its land for 20 ploughs, its serfs and villeins, its bordars and cottars. But Mells was to be caught up in the development which was slowly to change the face of the country. As we have seen by 1490, when New Street was built, Mells was a wealthy "townlet of clothing." The church stands as a reminder of this, and a chapel named after the patron saint of weavers, St Katherine, suggests that this was the main industry at the time. K G Ponting says that the greatest days of the weaving industry were between 1350-1400. The decline of the industry was a long drawn out one, and a pointer to this can be found in the parochial deeds. Among the signatures on a deed in 1684 there were 4 clothiers, 2 wooster makers, 1 cordwainer, and 1 broadweaver. In 1716, 6 clothiers, 1 weaver, and 1 tailor. In 1763 there is only 1 clothier, and 4 hosiers, and 1 cordwainer.

"In 1750 woad was largely cultivated in Mells, and there was in the parish a horse mill for grinding, and sheds for drying it, owned by Harvey the Woadman. Woad used in dyeing to form the ground of the indigo blue."[1] He is referred to elsewhere as "a well known character."*

It was in the 17th century that Henry Cornish, a Sheriff of London, carried on a clothing business in Mells, as did Richard Poyntz, an almost legendary figure.[2] The fact that he died in 1702 with a personal estate valued at £57.10.0. may be a pointer to the decline which had already set in. His son, who died in 1758, and described himself as a clothier of Mells, carried on the business after his father's death. There is a reference in the rate books to the effect that Widow Poyntz could not pay her rates in 1719, and a further reference to a payment to Widow Poyntz of 3/4 in 1724. The first Richard is said to have driven his coach and six.

There are references to weaving in the Churchwardens' Accounts: In 1710, "Paid for a Spinning Turn for Deborah Sweet, ls-l0d." In 1719: "Paid for Loome for Jno Hill £1-3-0." In the following year: "Paid Joseph Singer by order of ye Vestry 1lb 2s which was due to him for ye redemption of Issak Cook's Loom and upon ye account of taking his sister h. Singer from ye Parish." In 1831 there was a definite sign of the decline in the industry: "Josiah Young be allowed one pound to enable him and his family to remove to Chippenham where he expects to obtain

*Billingsley says that Harvey "was more generally known by the appellation of the Woadman, than by his own surname. Since his death it (the growing of woad) has been entirely discontinued" Agriculture of Somerset, 1797, 115 note.

Mells from Summer Leaze c1900

work as a weaver ... on condition that if he applies to this Parish in future . . . he shall continue in this Parish and work in agriculture."

The Census of 1831 does little to tell us how many weavers there were at that time. The population of Mells was 1259. Of these there were 127 employed in "the retail trade and handicraft." These are described as Masters, Shopmen, Journeymen and Apprentices. Of the wealthy clothiers there is no mention. The Parish now had only "twelve wholesalers, and capitalists, clergy, office clerks, professional and other educated men." By the time we have taken out the Squire, the Rector, the Doctor and the Fussells there is no room for many clothiers.

In that year there were 248 inhabited houses, two being built, and three uninhabited. In these houses there were 283 families. Employed in agriculture there were 94 families; in manufacture and trade 114; all other families, 75. In agriculture there were 11 first class farmers (yeomen), and 3 second class (small farmers) and 97 labourers. Manufacturers 3. Labourers (not agricultural) 33, other males over 20, 25. Servants; males over 20 years old, 8, under 20, 7. All female servants 34. Total population, male 614; female 645. Total, 1259.

The unemployment caused by the decline of the weaving industry was alleviated by the increase of the coal industry and the arrival of the Fussells in Mells. Collinson writing in 1791 said: "It is worthy of remark, that in this sequestered vale there are two iron forges, which at this period are carrying on a trade, little inferior, in point of extension,

Bilboa Mill

to those in the northern part of the kingdom. All western countries are supplied at these manufacturies with every iron implement of husbandry, and their connections extend to the European and American continents."[3]

"There are several coalworks in the parish, in some of which is a stratum of clay equal to the Stourbridge in the manufacture of crucibles; lead, manganese, pipeclay and fuller's earth, are also found there. In a hill called Vobster-Tor, from the hamlet of Vobster, is a vein of ash-coloured marble, streaked with red."[4] In 1798 there was calamine. "At the time a large quantity was raised in Mells, remarkably pure and of excellent quality."[5]

Coal mining was the oldest industry apart from weaving. In the reign of Charles II, Mells is mentioned among those places in "the forest of Mendipp where coalpits are." There is a reference to mining in the proceedings of the Court Leet and Court Baron of Mells. In 1665 an information of wrongs and trespasses said: "Gabriel Butcher and his

Brother John Butcher had landed and sold many sacks of cole on the marsh, your worshipp having no share thereof, and I being desirous to know the reason why they did so, they told me that I ought not to speak of it nor meddle with it." In 1678 land was leased with the clause "Except all Tymber Trees and Cole." The first mention in the Churchwardens' accounts is in 1757: "Received of William Watts for the free Share of Colls in the Catch Ground £1-15-0." This would be open cast coal. The pits at Vobster were in Lower Vobster. They were named Breach Pit, Old Pit and Little Pit. Leland wrote: "There cometh a brook from the coal pits of Mendip, and striketh by south into the bottom of Mells, and then runneth in Frome river." Drayton, in *Polyolbion* published in 1612, notes that:

"and Froome to her disgrace
Since scarcely ever washt the coalflek from her face;
But (melancholy grown) to Avon gets a path,
Through sickness forc't to seek for cure unto the Bath."

Wickham suggests that this refers to the coking works at Vobster and Egford. The Breach Pit was a coking works. The last pit was at Holwell Farm, Bilboa Pit. This finally closed in 1943.

William Page in his History of Somerset gives some interesting information. In 1836, children of 6 or 7 years old were employed at the pits. "Among the 100 hands at the Coal Barton and Vobster collieries in 1842 there were several. That in the Vobster series however gas is met and at Vobster, Edford and Newbury collieries safety lamps are used." There are miners still living who went down into the pits at 13 and 14, and who wore the guss and crook harness to draw the trucks of coal.

An amusing story is told which illustrates the difficulty the miners had in keeping clean. The Misses Horner were in the habit of entering the cottages without knocking. A miner had returned from the pit, and his wife had prepared his bath in the kitchen and gone out forgetting to lock the door. Suddenly the door opened and a Miss Horner appeared. One wonders whether the naked man or Miss Horner received the greater shock.

To introduce modern industry, which, in common with the whole of the Mendip area, is quarrying and its by-products, it is worth telling the story of the Beachims. Zebedee Beachim came to live at Lower Vobster Farm at the turn of the 19th century. The story comes from the Memoirs of Richard White: "Mr Zebedee Beachim of Lower Vobster was a great friend of my brother William. A son, William, from driving

Fussells Upper Works

an engine at Newbury Colliery, he became proprietor of two or more coalpits; there were large outputs; established large stone crushing works at Cranmore, supplying many thousands of tons of asphalted gravel and small stones for esplanades, pathways etc, both far and near, making a princely fortune." The name was later changed to Beauchamp, and the family became the leading mineowners in Somerset.

For the full story of the Fussells one must turn to Robert Atthill's *Old Mendip*. It is enough to say here that 56 men were employed in their edge tool works in the Iron Valley.* Before the end of the century the works were closed down. Rev J Skinner, of Camerton, in his diary gives us some idea of the conditions under which men worked. He had been to Nunney to buy a scythe: "We saw two men grinding scythes, with their noses literally at the grindstone ... we confine the people in bonds more heavy to be borne than any of the most cruel of Indian planters ever imposed on their property."

In a letter written to a relation in Australia c1865, William Long wrote: "Tell him that trade at the Mills is rather slacker now than when he left. James Fussell had the management of it for nearly three years. They have been making an inspection of the books for the last few days

*A rare plan of the Mells Iron Works about 1850, long lost to view in the vaults of the public offices, Frome, has recently been given to the Frome Society for Local Study by the late Rural District Council.

and they have found Mr Jessie has defrauded them in that short time of £700." One Francis Long, of the same family, and writing of what his father had told him, wrote: "Mells was a very busy place then. There were weavers in the Bottom and a lot of people worked at the Lower Iron Works at Wadbury Vale as well as the Upper Works."

As, until recent years, the upkeep of the roads was the responsibility of the local councils, there was in most parishes a quarry. The Parish quarry was at the crossroads at Vobster, and there was another quarry on either side of Limekiln Hill. The lime from the latter quarry was much sought after.

The Mendips have always been a source of great wealth. They have produced lead, coal, sheep, and latterly stone. In Fuller's *Worthies* it says of Bishop Still that he was well bestowed "and to have an unexpected blessing out of the entrails of the earth; I mean the lead mines of Mendip." Bishop Still married Jane Horner of Mells, "who drew with her a kind of alliance with Judge Popham, that swayed all temporall government of the countrie." Now today the wealth of Mendip is its stone. Whatley Quarry is in the Parish of Mells and in itself worth a fortune. No history of Mells in the future will be complete without reference to the Evemy brothers and their brother-in-law Mr Whitcombe. From a humble beginning these men made a fortune out of stone. Its by-product, cement, has also opened up what is comparatively a new industry; the works at Mells Road Station is a witness to this.

What remains of the abortive Dorset and Somerset Canal, and the railway are symbols of the effect progress has upon the lives and the investments of people in a developing world. Before the canal was finished the railway came; the motor car has closed the station. The quarries and the cement works are finding a new need for the railway for delivering fuel-oil and hauling long distance deliveries of stone.

From the Conquest to today the people of Mells have had to adapt themselves to change, and changes meant much suffering for many. The decline of the weaving trade was probably the worst time for the workers of Mells. In common with the rest of the country the relief of the poor reached huge proportions in the 18th and 19th centuries. Richard White says of this time: "Many a man out of work had to resort to poaching, which led to theft, ending in imprisonment and very often transportation. More men had been transported from Mells than from any other village of the same size."

Behind the changing character of all these industries there is of course agriculture. Here again nothing stood still. From the old manorial system of the open fields and the cottar with his rights and rotation of crops in the Common Fields, there grew up the yeoman farmer as he took possession of more holdings. It is possible that the enclosures of 1720, and the enclosing of the Park, completed the development and gave Mells something of its appearance today with its fields and hedges. Sheep gave way to corn. Dairy farming grew with the growth of the population of the country. In modern times machinery has taken the place of the farmworker.

One ancient institution was to suffer from the changes: the market which Abbot Monington had procured for Mells c1342. Richard White gives this description of it in the first half of the 19th century: "The fair at Mells was of considerable importance. As it was the only fair for sheep nearer than Wilton or Yarnborough Castle, the farmers of a considerable area supported it. I am not prepared to say how many sheep were penned; there must have been many thousand. The fair used to be held on Monday. A rough lot of men came on the Sunday to put up the booths, causing a great nuisance. Mr Horner had the fair put off to Tuesday. This proved the death blow to the fair. It struggled on for a few years and then gave up."

Fair Day was Michaelmas. The Vestry record shows that in 1833 "the sum of 15/- be paid by the Overseers on the Parish acct, towards paying the Constables employed to keep the peace during the Fair held last Michaelmas."

Michaelmas was also the time for the Harvest Thanksgiving which Prebendary Horner had introduced. No doubt the Rector felt that the "nuisance" was not the best thing for his Sunday morning congregation. The first Harvest Thanksgiving was held on Oct 2, 1842. The Prebendary became the Rector in 1836, and it would have been sometime towards the end of the first half of the century when the Fair ceased to function.

[1] Wickham, Spade & Terrier, 228
[2] Family of Poyntz, Maclean
[3] C H S, 11, 461
[4] ibid, 462
[5] V H S, 11, 391

THE VESTRY

Within most manors there was the Parish Church with its parson and churchwardens. These were responsible for the maintenance of the Parish Church and its services, and also the care of the poor. With any great change in the economic life of a community it is the poor who suffer most; and the poor you have always with you.

So in Mells there was, until 1826, the Court Leet responsible for roads, bridges, footpaths, drainage and the maintenance of law and order. The Courts Baron which defended the rights of the Lord of the Manor and the rights of the copyholders, and the Vestry with its responsibility for the church and the poor.

In 1826 the Select Vestry was set up which took over the work of the Court Leet. The Rector, Rev J F Doveton, J P made the first appointments to the Vestry: "all of whom were substantial Householders within the Parish of Mells." The Select Vestry continued until the formation of the Parish Council in 1894. The Churchwardens' Accounts tell the story of the work of the Vestry up to that time.

It was only natural that the care of the poor was a primary duty of the church. That it never worked successfully was due to the fact that the members of the church were everyman, and everyman has never been interested in the care of the poor. Before the dissolution of the monasteries, the travelling poor could get some help from them, but latterly many of them were so poor themselves they could do little about it; the care of the poor has always been haphazard. Yet our Welfare State has its roots in all that went before.

At the Reformation our Prayer Book only asked for one collection, and that is at the Communion Service. It was alms for the poor. The sentences preceding the collection read like "Give alms of thy goods and never turn thy face away from any poor man." But it was soon discovered that this appeal in itself was not enough. The Vestry was given power to levy a Poor Rate.

Giving alms has always been regarded as a christian virtue, and we find it practised down through the ages. Prior to the Reformation we have evidence that the people of Mells were not backward in the remembrance of the poor. John Diker, whose will was proved in 1503, left "to 20 poor persons, to each of them a sheet, to the poor all those shirts which are in my chest at Amesbury." John Robins in 1524 left "to 10 poor scolers of the gramer scole of Mells 3/4 each." A local priest made the rather strange bequest: "To every prisone in London, viz,

Newgate, Ludgate, The Benche and Marshallse, 20s ... to my parish church of Mells, £10." (Richard Woolman, 1528).

The Mells Charities are a reminder that from time to time there were those who left odd bits of land to the Church and Parish for the benefit of the poor and the maintenance of the church. Most of this was given after the Reformation. There was also an Almshouse on the south side of the river on the piece of land which runs along the river between Wadbury and the Limekiln bridge. This was the gift of John Horner in 1592. "The Alms House and Church House for the poor and the Church." These premises had either been allowed to fall into a state of disrepair or were no longer large enough by 1708. In that year "Thomas Jefferies and Richard Moore. churchwardens of the parish of Mells, did pay unto William Jeffres of the said parish the sum of three pounds and tenn shillings for his house at the ffut of Haidon hill ffor the building of an Almshouse. . . Deliver into the hand of above said William Jeffres the House called Bartletts which Richard Clark had **...** to keep Repos and in Joy for himself during the term of his natural life yealding and paying one piper come a yeare."

Another entry tells us where the money for the building came from: "Recd, a poore rate which was given by the parish to us, it being the which money, with the overbalance of the year . . . the consent of the parish Lent to the use of the poore toward the building of the Almshouse." Plus Rate, £23-12-9. Donations, £40-11-6. Thos Horner £25. The Almshouse cost about £120, including "ye massons work £11-14-8" and for "a thousand of board and carriage £5-6-6." It still stands and was built to house four men and four women.

As the unemployment problem grew there came the workhouse. The deed describes it: "house, court and orchard situated on Mells Green late in the tenure of Thomas Whatley . . . upon trust . . . for a house or place for the reception maintenance and employment of the poor of the parish of Mells, and a person or persons to reside in the said tenement or Dwelling House for the better ordering and taking care of the poor to be placed therein, and to no other use, or intent or purpose whatsoever." (1763/4).

Extracts of the Workhouse Accounts give us some idea of the scope of its activities, and an insight into costs and of a primitive form of transport. The inmates were expected to work, and in 1813 the receipts from work done were £40. Against this there was an account

The Duckery, Mells Park (Old Manor Mill)

for flour of £80. The following entries are taken from the whole period of the existence of the Workhouse.

A shirt for Pool, 3/8. Mr Charles for a sheet, 5/-. Breeches for Pool, 2/6. Turnip seed 4d. Cabbage seed 4d. Farmer Barnes for a fat pig, £2-5-0. Widow Ashman a shift and making, 3/3. Clothing four children, 17/8. 300 fagots £1-10-0. Lucy Dodimead for shaving 6/3. Wm Long's shoes, 5/10. 60 pounds of Beef, at 2½ pd, 12/6. 300 of plants, 3/8. 40lbs of veal, 8/4. 20 yards of Linsey £1-11-3. 30lbs Bacon 18/9. Mutton for broth Mary Griffin, 1/-. Delivering Betty Clements, 1/6. For a carving knife. 1/6. Mr Charles for Malt and Hopts, £17-6-8½. A bed pan for the Workhouse, 10d. Paid Thos Horler, 21 horseload of cole at 1/4 p horse, £1-8-0. Sack of turnips 2/6. A garden hoe 1/2. The work would appear to include gardening and the brewing of beer. The bedpan suggests the care of the aged sick, and the delivery of Betty Clements that unmarried mothers were housed here.

In 1825 Joseph Cole was the Master of the Workhouse, and had his salary reduced from "£12 p ann to £8 p ann." The following year Thomas White was "appointed Foreman of Mells Parish roads, also he and his wife to be Governor and Governess of the Workhouse at a salary of £14 pr annum with an addition of £1 at the years end provided it be done to the satisfaction of his employers. Their son Benjamin to continue with his parents."

The extent of the power the Vestry held over the poor is seen from the following:

"That Elizabeth Hinton with her two illegitimate children be not allowed to leave the Workhouse.

"That John Himan and his wife be removed from the Workhouse to the Almshouse as soon as possible.

"That the present system of maintaining and clothing paupers in a Workhouse in this parish be discontinued at Midsummer next and allow them as a substitute a regular Weekly allowance of cash." Apparently the Workhouse was not always full, for in 1828 it was agreed "that Colonel Horner shall take that part of the Workhouse unoccupied by this Parish." With the Union of parishes for the care of the poor the Workhouse closed down in 1837. The house was converted into six cottages and continued as such until recent times. The house has now been renovated and makes two attractive dwellings.

Meanwhile there were those who needed care who found no place in the Workhouse. The help given them differs over the years, and increases as the time goes on. The only reference to the poor in 1660, the date of the first churchwardens' records, is impersonal: "Distributed to souvrall poor as by a note of pticulars Doth appear, £1-13-0," and "received at the fast which also was distributed to the poor. £1-13-0." Mention had already been made of assistance given to travellers passing through Mells. In the earlier days more was given in this direction than to the poor of the parish. The kind of assistance given will appear from the following extracts from the various records:

William Lauds shroud and making his grave and to those that carried him to Church, 6/2.

Gave to Henry Sweet to help him in his Nesesotie, 10/6. Gave to old William Clarke in his weakness, 4/-.

1665. Paid for 2 shirts for Amy Large's Sonne, 4/-.

It is not until 1701 that there is a Mells Poor Rate and Disbursement Book, and this widens the field of relief to cover apprentices. These had to be fitted up before being taken over by their masters, and in 1704 there was "bought at norton faire peeces of Narah Cloth, one 29 yards at ls 9d ye yard £2-6-8.

ditto one 28 yards at 1/8 ye yard £2-6-8.

ditto for carriage home 7d."

A month later: "To daniel Maggs for making Eight sheets for boys apprentist by Mr Barges and Truckwell, and cloth of him for too sheets moore and for fourteen Ells Nollen for Cravatts and burial dress for goody Rogers, and 2 shurts for prentis boys £3-15-4."

In 1706 there is the complete setting up of a boy. "Expenses at the Inn when James Coocks boy was bound apprentice, 3/4½.

Paid in money with the boy the sume of £2-0-0.

paid daniol mags for 5 yards of Cloth for ye boy, 10/10.

for triming for the suit and a shirt and a cravat, 13/7.

for a pair of stockens, 1/8.

paid John hakins for making the 2 suits, 8/11.

paid John porry for to pair of shows, 4/11.

paid Thomas naish for a hatt, 2/0.

paid John Chilton for the indentures, 5/-."

In 1707, "allowed him (the Rector) for clothing his parish boy £1."

There is one strange entry in 1709: For badges for the Poor, 20 at 3d p peece, 5/-.

In 1710 an apprentice girl is fitted up. Paid for a Hatt, A Marto and petecoat and Two Aprons, Two Caps a fillet two Neck cloths, Two pair of Stockings, A pair of Boffice and Stomacher for Mr Mompersions Apprentice, £1-8-7.

There were 26 people in receipt of weekly pay in 1721.

In that year "Wolling and Liney bought to distribute to the poor for making clothes, also druggett 38 yds, £2-1-2, blanketing 47 yrds, 4/8.

Bell, Woll, Beer, Laying out of Needs Child, 3/6. Lent a poor man by the Colonel's order, 10/-.

John Clements house rent £1-1-0.

John Coles for 20 weeks keeping of Jane Gibbons at 3/6 p.w.

For a frock for Gibbons 5/8."

Relief was only given if there was a residentiary qualification. If a person died in another parish then it was up to the home parish to bring the body back for burial. "The Widow Hodges, paid for coffin 8/-, Wool 1/0, ye grave bell 2/-, for drink at ye burial 3/-, for horse to Trowbridge 1/- expenses 1/-.

For fetching widow William's goods back 3/-.

1715. Paid John Coles for 2 sacks of coal, one ye widow Cook, and one to Wm Jefers, 2/2.

That Berry Eastwood to have a pair of shoes before the Winter sets in."

A note of appreciation: "That a present of £1 be made to Joseph Brown as a reward for maintaining a numerous family without parochial assistance."

"That G N Hancox ... in future occupy a house belonging to Mr Beachim, and the annual rent of 30/- to be paid by Mells Parish."
"That the Parish pay George Cole's rent during his illness, 2/- p w"
The fate of any who needed relief but did not belong to the Parish is illustrated by the following entry: "That John French be examined and immediately removed from the Parish."
A number of families must have left Mells in search of work in the developing North. There are several letters in the Rectory which appeal for help for those who have fallen on bad times, and one in particular which states that the applicants are near starvation, but that if Mells will promise to reimburse any relief given they would make immediate payments.

Much has been said of the harshness of those times, but there are signs too that there was a certain amount of humanity shown. In 1833, one John Gane, (probably he had been a parish apprentice) was living at Paulton and had a wife and six children. He was a Mells parishioner and was therefore entitled to ask Mells for assistance. His request was an unusual one. He was a blacksmith; he had worked 10 years with his master, now dead, and had an offer of the business "according to the request of the principle inhabitants of Paulton, that the Stock in Trade, Tools etc, are valued at the sum of £22, and that of himself he is not able to advance that sum, he therefore solicits of Mells Parish a loan of £15. Agreed, the said Stock in Trade, Tools etc, be received as the property of this Parish until the sum of £15 be repaid."

Towards the end of the 18th century the need for better roads was recognised. The Turnpike system had improved many of the major roads, but there were other roads which needed repair and also Church paths, many of which ran alongside the Turnpike roads. Who better than the poor to repair these roads? As early as 1832 the Vestry had decided to repair the road between Hawthorn Cross and Babington Lodge, a road maintained by The Buckland Turnpike Trust, rather than pay the Trust £6. In 1849 the Parish decided to appoint a paid surveyor at the salary of £10 p a. The first to be appointed was Zebedee Beachim. When in 1866 the Radstock Turnpike Trust wrote to the Vestry asking for the rateable value of the parish and the Highway Rate, they also asked whether the Vestry was in favour of the abolition of the Trust. The

Mells c1900

answers were, that the Rateable Value was £5458-14-4, the Highway Rates and that they were in favour of the abolition of the Trust. It would seem that the parish was beginning to feel that it was better to employ its own poor on the repair of the roads than rely upon the turnpike system.

In 1826, it was agreed: "That should any person employed on the Parish road refuse to work for any of the Paymasters at the same wages he receives on the Parish road he is no longer to be employed on the Parish road." The Paymasters were the substantial residents of Mells such as the Lord of the Manor, the Rector, the Fussells, and the farmers. The first jobs done are very modest. "Agreed that the Church Wardens do repair the Church path called Drums Hill." (1826). In 1825: "that a pitched footway, 4½ feet wide be made across the road at the south end of New Street." This is still there. There was a foreman: "That Tradua Ashman's pay of 9/- pr.week be reduced to 7/- pr week, he not agreeing to the same quits their service as foreman of the parish roads on Saturday next." A week or two later: "That Thomas White be appointed Foreman of Mells Parish roads also he and his wife to be Governor and Governess of the Workhouse."

The following extracts tell their own story:
"That persons employed on the Parish roads shall not be allowed for parts of a day's work, i e for ½ or ¼ of a day's work."
"That John Jones who is at present working on the Parish roads be

allowed a pair of shoes and his wages of 3/6 pr week be reduced to 2/6 pr week.

"That John Fook (who has been receiving 3/- pr week from this Parish) shall be set to work on the Parish roads.

"That James Biggs shall not receive further relief from this Parish unless he come to work.

"That Richard Barry's two sons shall be employed on the Parish roads until further employment be found for them.

"That Labourers employed on the Parish roads shall work Saturdays as other days.

"That Wm Hoddinott, Thos Coles, Edward Hambleton or any others having a wife only be paid 4/- pr week when they work by the week on the roads."

One great improvement was made in the roads at this time. In 1828: "This Parish unanimously agrees to advance Eighty pounds towards the New Bridge and road in this Parish on condition that Col Horner will be at all other expenses in making said new bridge and road completely. Col Horner taking Drums Bridge wholly into his own possession."

The old road ran from Tents Hill down to the river, along the Doctor's Walk, to the building at the foot of Drums Hill, and then over the mill stream and river. The New Bridge is the present bridge at the bottom of Tents Hill. The final proposal was: "Col Horner having made a proposal to build a new bridge over the Mells river and a new arch over the Mill Stream below Drums Bridge and to complete the road and fence wall that may be necessary, on condition that the Parish give him 65 guineas, the stone quarried on Tents Hill and two days hauling. The Vestry unanimously agreed."

In 1840, prior to the building of Wadbury House, Mr Thomas Fussell submitted to the surveyors of Mells that a pathway "leading out of the public highway from Mells to Great Elm through and over certain enclosed lands called Grass Wadbury and Ploughed Wadbury, the property of Thomas Strangways Horner Esquire, and now in the occupation of him, the said Thomas Fussell as tenant thereof and terminating in the said Parish of Mells at other enclosed lands called Little Furlong at the commencement of the Parish of Great Elm in this county, the property of Thomas Williams as Lessee for lives under Sir Henry Strachey Bt, and which said highway so proposed to be stopped up as unnecessary contains in the said Parish of Mells in length eight hundred and five yards or thereabouts and in breadth three feet or thereabouts upon a medium. Resolved . . . that the proposal of Mr Thomas Fussell to stop up the same as unnecessary be accepted by the Vestry on his undertaking to widen the present road from Mells to Great Elm to twenty feet, (throughout the Parish of Mells)."

In the same year, at a Public Vestry it was decided to close "as unnecessary a certain public highway called Almshouse Hill or Almshouse Road situated within the said Parish and leading from Mells to Whatley in the County of Somerset commencing at Mells Almshouse extending up the said hill called Almshouse Hill and terminating at Haydon Crossways. The road was 20ft wide and the Vestry reserved thereout a bridle or halter path of the width of five feet throughout the whole".

Harvest time brought some relief to the rates:
"That James Jones family pay of 7/- p week to be reduced to 5/- p week during the harvest.

May Cook's pay of 1/6 p w be discontinued during the harvest." Finally there is the direction of labour to the Paymasters:
"That Cornelious Harder be employed by Mr Jno Feaver for one year from Lady Day last at 2/- pr Week."

The Care of the Sick.
The first mention of a doctor is in 1706: "Paid the doctor Compton for weekley pay £4-0-0." In the same year: "Paid for blooding Jane Gibbon and mending her shoes, 10d." Other references show that the official doctor was not the only one used.
1715: "Gave the dockter woman for ye widow Copers child 1/-."
1718: "Gave Jno Blacker to by Lances to Bleed with 4/0. Gave Hester Perry 2 weeks of sickness, 2/-.
Paid ye midwife for John Dodimeads wife, 2/-.
Paid Mrs Moore for curing Nathaniel Philip's wife's leg, 12/-.
1718. Paid Wm Laver for Dr Nicholas attending John Naish's wife £2-15-0.
To ye widow Harris in ye smallpox, 9/-.
1741. Gave the Wid Dore to make ointment to Cure Need's Children of the Ech, 1/-."
By 1826 a Club was in existence and "Wm Nuth who has a wife and three children under 8 years of age be allowed three shillings pr week during his illness, taking his weekly pay from ye Club of 6/- at two thirds, ie 4/- p week." In 1831, it was resolved: "that John Pope be

allowed 3/- p week for six weeks from the 2nd August next at Salisbury so as to receive the benefit of the Infirmary there."

Mr Thomas Allen was appointed in 1826, with "annual Salary of sixteen pounds sixteen shillings as Medical Attendant for the Parish not including Midwifery and Casualties etc." Very soon after it was decided that: "Mr Allen, Surgeon, be not allowed for visits to any pauper patient belonging to Mells Parish without a previous order from the Overseers for that purpose." Another entry is: "That Caleb Long be not in future allowed anything towards paying for surgical operations, i e tapping his wife for the Dropsy."

Mr White, in his memoirs, tells us that in his young days "Mr Drake was the village doctor. There were a lot of one-legged men in Mells. When anything was the matter with a leg, Dr Drake was for having it off, as in that case it was a perfect cure. He was the Parish Doctor and could charge 3 guineas for operating on a pauper." Hospitals are mentioned as early as 1718: "Richard Poyntz, Hospital money, 14/11. Thomas Naish's Hospital money, £1-2-11." This would appear to be the hospital at Salisbury.

In 1832 a meeting of the Vestry was held "for the purpose of establishing a Board of Health in the Parish of Mells, to inspect and to abate or remove all nuisances that may be injurious to the health of the public . . . Col Horner having kindly offered Kingsdown Farm as a hospital (in the event of the Parish being afflicted with Cholera)."

One development in the care of the poor was the founding of the Friendly Societies. That at Mells was established in 1844, and the Founder Members were The Rector, Preb J S H Horner, Rev W Blackwell, the Curate, and John Fussell, with Francis Long as the Clerk. Contributions were paid at the rate of 8¾d pr month for a youth of 15, graduating to 4/- pr month for a man of 50. The sick benefits were 4/- a week for the first 12 weeks and 2/- a week "during the affliction." At 65 a member received 4/- pr week for life, but no sick benefits. A member could hold up to 2½ shares; e g he could make a double contribution and receive double benefits. There was a payment at death to the next of kin of £4. The Annual Meeting was held on Whit-Monday at 10 o'clock and: "The members so disposed shall walk in procession to the Church; after Divine service the business of the Society shall be transacted." No allowances were paid for V D or accidents caused by intoxication, profligacy, quarrelling or fighting, and "if the death of a member be caused by the sentence of law or by his own hand, the sum which would otherwise be due . . . shall be forfeited."

The Friendly Societies were a step away from the stigma of being "on the Parish" and towards our present Social Security. The care of the poor passed from the Vestry to the Board of Guardians, and in 1895 there were eight inmates from Mells in the Frome Union; 4 imbeciles, 1 orphan (aged 12), 1 confinement, 1 illness, and 1 infirm. There were 25 married couples or single persons getting relief. Of these 18 were for old age, 2 were widows with young children, 3 were sick, one bedridden, and one with a broken leg. The eldest was Mary Cook who was 92 with Joseph Ruddick and his wife as runners up at 89. The rateable value of Mells was £6212, it had a population of 953, and relief given over six months was £104-2-6¾.[1]

[1] Frome Guardians' Report, 1895

The White Bridge c1900, the cottage has been demolished and a new timber bridge in a similar style was opened in April 2012

EDUCATION

The village school as we have known it is not an old establishment. Education was not very much sought after in earlier days, not even by the rich. The Tudor kings and queens and their children had a good education, and at that time there were signs of a growing desire for more. The Vestry was supposed to cater for a school. In Mells there was a Grammar School in 1524, when John Robyns left 10/- to the schoolmaster, and 3/4 each to 10 poor scholars of the Grammar School.

John Horner in 1592 granted the Almshouse and Church House for the use of the poor and the Church. A year or two later the lease was altered to read that the Church House was to be used as a school "as it was then used, and that the Upper Rooms in it as a lodging for the Schoolmaster." A map of Mells dated 1680 shows a school in a building at Rectory Corner, near the bus shelter. This was one of a group of houses known as Twaddle Alley.* It would seem that the school had a checkered history, and it is probable that the number mentioned in John Robyn's will, ten, was the average number of children at one time. When we remember that as late as 1836 children of six and seven were still being employed in the pits, there was little time for education.

The beginning of the 19th century marks a great forward movement towards the education of the poor and of the middle classes. As always the Lord of the Manor was involved. Colonel Horner leased the present school and school house to the National Society, about 1813, for as long as it was used for educational purposes.

At first the school was the older part of the present one, believed to have been a weaving room, with the house as the residence of the head teacher. Mells school was one of the first five church schools in Somerset. There were in those early days about 100 children attending, but of course the attendance was not compulsory, and it is probable that most of them left by the time they were ten years of age.

It was felt that there was need of a separate boys' school, and Colonel Horner built the Boys' School in New Street in 1840. This school was capable of taking 150 children.[1] Queen Victoria's head was a jubilee addition to the building and was carved by Edwin Long, one of the Longs of Mells, who also carved the panels in the Music Room

*There was also a Twaddle or Twattle Alley in Frome between Gentle Street and Blindhouse Lane. In both cases the name is derived from *tote,* an Anglo-Saxon word for a look-out place, or beacon.

at Berkely Towers in Cheshire. There was now a boys' school and a girls' school. This was to give the name to the Boys' and Girls' Crossing on the Vobster road. Here the boys and girls from Vobster parted on their way to school. Vobster had its own Infants' School at Frogbury Cottage. In 1889 the boys' school had an average attendance of 60, the Girls' and Infants' School on the Green 84, and the school at Vobster, 23. This was before education was compulsory.

The education of the masses had its social problems. The farmers and tradesmen did not necessarily want their children to go to the same school as their workers. At the same time any idea of sending them away to a boarding school had not entered their minds. In Mells there were private schools springing up in response to the desire to keep them apart. We get some information from Richard White. He was born in 1828 and did not go to school until he was eight years old. "This was to a day school for middle class boys kept by Mr Joseph White. (No relation). His sister also kept a school for girls under the same roof. His brother Samuel and his mother carried on a general shop adjoining . . . Mr Joseph White was a first class teacher. Boys came from far and near. It was the fashion to flog boys for not saying their lessons properly or for any dereliction of duty. For anything of a graver character a good birching." After three years Mr White gave up and went to Weston-super-Mare where he gained distinction as an architect and surveyor.

"Another school was shortly afterwards opened at Prospect Cottage by Misses Alword and Tuck. This was a middle class school. Miss Alword taught the boys and Miss Tuck the girls. Robert and I attended this school for two years or more until it was given up. Another was soon started on the same premises under the auspices of Rev J S H Horner, Miss Saunders being the presiding genius. The teaching at this school was quite novel. We were taught mental arithmetic. We were taught to write by dictation on the painted walls with chalk, afterwards being questioned as to its meaning. . . We were taught history by Little Arthur's History of England, which was a very pleasant way of learning it. We were taught geography in a pleasant way by drawing sketches on the wall of what we could remember. . . Chief towns were also impressed on our memories, in this way. We were also taught singing by Hullah's Sol-fa system."

Prebendary Horner is very much in the picture now. As Richard was too old to reap any further benefit from his education at this school, the Rector had him at the Rectory for a couple of hours a day, several days in the week. "He taught me geometry, land measuring, a little drawing, besides our reading together on a variety of subjects." After a time Richard graduated to a school in Frome run by Rev W M H Williams in Cork Street.

Prebendary Horner's most outstanding enterprise was the foundation of St Andrew's College in the Manor House. It was opened on the Feast of the Conversion of St. Paul, 1848. The college diary relates that at its opening the "prayers were said by Rev W M Blackwell in the presence of the Archdeacon Merriman, the Rural Dean, Rev Dr Griffiths and other clergy." That the object was: "A society which takes the Prayer Book for its rule, and which will endeavour to carry out faithfully all that it enjoins, and requires the Warden and Fellows undertake the care of the students, not for any desire of worldly gain or advancement, but as a good work in which they are happy to be employed."

"The students are admitted with the understanding that their training is with a view to make them useful members of Christ's Holy Catholic Church ... it is hoped that within these walls youths go forth to undertake duties of Schoolmasters at home or Missionaries abroad; at least their general training here will be in this direction." The staff were not to take vows as it was not to be a community but a college.The College "received as its inmates those who could not reasonably expect to be members of the Houses of our Universities . . . now with an immensely increased population and with an intelligent middle class loudly calling for instruction it seems that such houses as this are wanted to secure to them a sound religious education."

The first Warden was Wm Moberley and the first Fellows were Wm Greenstock, Wm Cowley and Henry Theophilus Monk. The Bursar was Rev Wm Blackwell. It is to its earlier days that one must place the two material benefits the College gave to the parish: its stained glass and its pew-ends. Mr Blackwell taught the Horwood brothers the art of glass burning, and Rev Edmund Stansfield taught the Clarke brothers the art of woodcarving. It is interesting to note that in the early days an agricultural class was also added to the curriculum. Also that it was not long before this latter set of boys no longer ate with the rest.

By 1853, Edwin Horwood was referred to as "our village artist." In that year he set up a window which is now the south window of the chancel and has the date scratched on it. While he was in Manchester in 1857 at an exhibition of stained glass, the works were removed from the Rectory to the Manor. Before Edwin left Mells to set up business in Frome, he had sent glass to many churches all over England and two to Sydney in Australia. In Mells itself we see the peak of his art in the north window of the chancel, a memorial to his teacher, Rev Wm Blackwell, and which dates from 1882. The Horwood brothers opened their business in Bridge Street, Frome, and in 1889 were still in business at 20 Christ Church Street West. Mr Blackwell appears to have left Mells in 1861. He was appointed Rector of Cloford by Prebendary Horner in 1864, but resigned a year later and died in 1866. Of this period, when the stained glass industry was in its infancy, E Liddall Armitage wrote: "Considering the limitations of the period it should be recognised as a fine pioneering achievement."

Of the Clarke brothers and Mr Stansfield, their memorial in Mells is the pew-ends, and Mr Stansfield had an additional memorial in the church at Vobster. We are told that: "Mr Stansfield offered to subscribe £1000 to the building of a church in the hamlet due west of the village on condition that it should be dedicated to his Patron Saint, Edmund, King and Martyr and that he should be allowed to do all the carved work himself. This was agreed to and the small Church was built by the architect Ferrey under the inspiration of Merton College, Oxford."[2]

I have been told that Rev George Horner used to tell people that all the heads sculptured there were of men connected with the building, and that he could put a name to each one. The Church was consecrated on Nov 1, 1848 by the Bishop of Bath and Wells "who preached to 100 communicants." It is interesting to note that the Clarks also carved the pew-ends in Kilkhampton Church in Cornwall for Lord John Thynne.

Mr Stansfield was an interesting person; he was an Ensign of the 51st Regiment of Foot and later Lieutenant. As a lieutenant he made two voyages to Tasmania in a sailing ship, in charge of convicts on both occasions. Whilst there he dined with the Governor, and Arctic Explorer, Sir John Franklin.

Dr Corfield, of Rustington, wrote in a letter to *The Times* on February 17, 1961: "Edmund Stansfield was a carver in stone and wood of great merit, a musician of no mean order, and a painter. It was while he was painting the Crucifixion that he died suddenly; the painting is in Rustington Church." He died in 1907 having left Mells in 1856.

Mells School about 1905

It is impossible to say how much the College accomplished in its short life. Odd notes in the diary tell us little but may be a fair account of the sort of thing that followed any connection with the College. Mr D Romeston was ordained in 1843; Jas Rower went on to East Brent Training College. Mr Wm Cowley, organist and choirmaster, having been nominated by Sir Wm Codrington, after visiting the College, went out to Antigua and was ordained by the bishop there. On March 5, 1858, Rev J Bamforth left for Gravesend to embark in the steamer *Golden Fleece* as chaplain to troops proceeding to Calcutta. He was to work in Ceylon.

The last warden was Rev H Twells. "Of him it is said that upon hearing of a better central position, persuaded all the clerical students to follow him to London, and the whole affair collapsed." Whether or not this is entirely true one cannot say. It could be that the upkeep of the college was more than the Rector could afford. To Mr Twells we owe the hymn, *At even ere the sun was set,* and several others.

Although the College was not a community in the accepted sense of the word, the day of a student was very similar to that of a monk. The day began at 6 a m and proceeded as follows: 6.45, prayers, 7.30, study, 7.45, breakfast, 8.30, divine service. The morning's work and study ended at 12 o'clock with prayers. The student returned to study at 2 o'clock. Twice a week there was music in church. Divine Service was at 5, followed by more study and prayers at 8.30 and supper at 9 o'clock. In 1853 there were 6 men in residence, 10 boys, and a staff of 3 women and 3 girls with 6 agricultural boys. The income appears to have come from a curate who paid £50 p a and four others who paid £25 each; boys' fees at £50 p a with visitors paying 10/- p w. The Rector provided the house rent and tax free and undertook the repairs. The Rector also provided the service of the house which consisted of the Dame, Margaret Trussler, Letitia James, and the labour of the agricultural boys. This was in 1858. With the departure of Mr Twells the house closed down and the Manor House was let to Rev J R Fussell. One interesting sideline is that at all festivals the aged were entertained to tea, about 10 persons, and on St Andrew's Day there was a dinner for 60.

Like the glassmaking, St Andrew's College can be looked upon as a fine pioneering achievement, a forerunner of the teachers' training colleges and perhaps of the agricultural college. Prebendary Horner was a keen agriculturalist and attended the Agricultural Show regularly. In one of his letters to his wife when on such a visit he expresses the fear that steam would soon replace the horse on the land.

For many years Mrs Martha Cook[3] (1802-1894) kept a Dame School at no 2 Garston Cottage, where the school was an extension to the cottage. A peep-hole was cut in the door between the living room and school so she could keep an eye on the children while preparing a meal. The peep-hole was still there in 1976.

The passing of the Education Acts of more recent years have changed the character of our education. There are no longer any private schools for the education of the middle classes in Mells; the boys' school in New Street has been closed for a long time; the new classroom at the present school was built as a last ditch attempt to keep the school for boys and girls of all ages, but the post war development has left Mells with a Junior School serving several villages.

[1] Kelly's Directory 1889
[2] Jekyll
[3] L D Redfarn, personal communication 1976

RELIGION IN MELLS

No one knows when the first church was built in Mells but by that time the Latin Mass would have been the main service of the day. The people were to hear Mass on Sunday and on the major Feast Days. There was a close link in the early days with the religious houses. The Abbot of Glastonbury was the Lord of the Manor as well as being the Patron of the Living. Richard Beere visited his relations here; he was a Carthusian monk, and the Abbot's nephew, and Mrs Pike, of Samuels, was a niece. John Diker, in his will, left to Lady Katherine Diker, Prioress of Amesbury, "one gold ring, and to Lady Joan Horner of the same convent one small maser." Lady Joan was at some time the sub-prioress[1]. This close link with the Church of so many of the clothiers and other wealthy residents of the parish, would suggest that any change such as the Reformation was to bring to many parts of Europe, would not touch this small townlet in Somerset. But the change did come and it was felt in Mells. Not only did Henry VIII break off relations with the Pope, but he also introduced the "vulgar tongue" into the Mass. It was not until Edward VI that the whole of our services were in English. There was "The Supper of the Lord, and Holy Communion commonly called the Mass." Queen Mary reintroduced the Latin Mass for a time but after Elizabeth I, English became the recognised language for our services.

During the Commonwealth the Prayer Book was prohibited and all prayers were extempore. After the Restoration the Prayer Book was re-introduced and has remained the only legal book for the Church of England until recent times. In 1660 the Churchwardens paid: "For a new Common prayer book and carrige, 10/6", and in 1662: "for a Communion Book and the fetchin of him, 9/-." With the Reformation came the sermon or the preaching of the Word. For many years these were of considerable length. There were no hymns at first and little music.

In 1710 there is a reference to a gallery in the church. "Layed out towards the Gallery, £10." Where this gallery was is not known, but it was probably under the tower. This gallery was erected before the Evangelical Revival when so many galleries were erected, and suggests that it was for the use of a choir and or a band.

It is not until 1779 that there is any mention of music. That year the Churchwardens paid: "Willm Strode for Music Books for the use of the Gallery, £1-1-0," and at a Vestry held the 15 April 1788 it was "agreed that the Gallery be altered and appropriated for the singers and the School." Edwin F Long, in his memoirs, wrote of the early years of the 19th century: "The Curate read the Psalms and Prayers. The Glorias were sung as well as the *Te Deum* and *O be joyful,* to double chants, and the Quire of Men and Women often sang Anthems as we sat and listened to them. Your Uncle James played the Base Viol when he did not play the Flute, and Mr George Smith the clarionet. There were fiddles, and Oboe and Flutes. The Clerk would say 'Let us sing to the glory of God the Old Hundreth Psalm,' and then the band would play the tune and young and old would sing."

The next stage is that which developed into what was to continue until recent times. Richard White tells us that Prebendary Horner made many changes and that "an organ soon found its way into the church and a small choir. . . The Clerk's services were no longer required to make the responses and the sexton was also relieved of his duty of walking around in the church to preserve order and gently tapping on the head those who were nodding; with a sharper tap for those who were snoring."

The beginning of the 19th century marked the peak of the Evangelical Revival and the beginning of the Tractarian or Catholic Movement in the Church of England. It was the latter which was to affect the worshippers in the church. The reaction of the Puritans to the ritual of the Church before the Reformation had had a great influence upon worship. Simplicity was the norm. The services were taken in cassock and surplice with hood and scarf. The sermon was preached in a preacher's gown. Holy Communion was celebrated only four times a year at the greater festivals. This latter, not so much from neglect, as from a sincere desire to protect the Sacrament from being treated too lightly.

The Tractarians felt that the Prayer Book intended that the Communion Service should have a more central place in the worship of the Church, and that simplicity had been carried too far. They thought a certain amount of ritual was a help rather than a hindrance to worship. The Service Registers tell the story of the development of the Church's worship during the 19th century. The registers began in 1841. In that year on Christmas day there were 51 communicants; on Easter Day 72. The Harvest Thanksgiving was held for the first time on Oct 2; on that day there were 50 communicants. There was also the "first experiment with our new and young choir." For the first time there was a celebration of Holy Communion on Ascension Day with 41 communicants, and a monthly Communion was started. Psalms were chanted. This was probably the introduction of plainsong, which was sung in Mells for about 50 years.

The new rector had much support for his innovations. On Feb 1, 1846 there were 100 communicants at the monthly Communion. In May there was a Confirmation of 280 candidates of whom 138 were from Mells and 111 from Leigh, which at that time was linked with Mells. Another innovation was that in that year a sermon was preached in a surplice. Evensong was moved from the afternoon to the evening for the convenience of the labouring class, and by the end of the year there was a full choral service. St Andrew's House was opened in 1848 and on Easter Day there were 127 communicants at a full choral service. The choir was now well established; S Cook had a full choral service for his funeral, and the choir took part in a festival at Wells.

At Vobster the Chapel of St Edmund's was consecrated by the Bishop of Bath and Wells on All Saints' Day 1848. There were 100 communicants. The first "early Communion" was in 1849 and there were 42 communicants. A Fast Day during the cholera scare brought 75 communicants to church. By 1854 the Easter Communicants numbered 200. Hymns Ancient and Modern was introduced in 1869. When the Rector died there was a Requiem with 21 communicants. The first reference to the Three Hours' Service was on Good Friday 1883, and in that year the Feast of St Peter was not observed because of the Commemoration of Bishop Ken at Wells.

Some idea of Prebendary Horner's successful ministry can be got from the figures recorded in 1852. The morning congregation was 156; the afternoon 78; the evening, 230, and the morning Sunday School had 272 children and the afternoon school 96.

It was during the incumbencies of the two Horners that the worship took on the outward appearance that was to be the norm of most parish churches. Although they were both Tractarians, vestments were not introduced until about 1940. The rectors who followed them were moderate churchmen, and no great changes were to follow until the introduction of the present experimental Services. The music at Mells continued at a high standard for many years. During Canon Hannay's incumbency Evensong was broadcast from the church, and members of the choir took part in a Musical Festival arranged by the Royal School of Church Music, in the Albert Hall.

In a parish like Mells it was difficult for Non-Conformity to find a place. Until recent years the Manor would employ only Anglicans, and as all the land was owned by the Lord of the Manor or the Rector it was

St Dominic's Chapel in Mells Manor Garden   *A R Yeates*

difficult for any other church to find a plot of land upon which to build. The Wesleyans made a great effort. John Wesley visited Mells, in September 1785[2], and it was then he put on record: "Tues 6 I preached at Paulton and Coleford; Wed 7th, in an open place, near the road to Mells. Just as I began, a wasp, though unprovoked, stung me upon the lip: I was afraid it would swell, so that to hinder my speaking, but it did not. I spoke distinctly, nearly two hours in all; and was no worse for it."

E W F Long's manuscript states: "The Wesleyan Preachers, full of zeal, came to Mells holding meetings at Woodlands End. Soon many iron workers were converted, and Mr Thos Fussell seeing their changed mode of life, became interested in the movement and joined it. He got a lease of land, close to where was to be our home, and father told me the chapel was built in six weeks. Mr Fussell, of Wadbury House, used to ride in his carriage every Sunday morning and evening to the services as long as he lived."

Richard White says that the chapel was an upper room fitted up as a chapel. This was at the rear of the cottages at Woodlands End. The large iron gates erected at the entrance were taken away for scrap during the last war. In 1876 the lease fell in and the Methodists were left without a home. For some time they held open air and cottage meetings, but no site for a chapel could be found. At Vobster they had better success and a chapel was built in 1898. In 1922 another effort resulted

War Memorial,designed by Sir Edward Lutyens   *Peter Lowry*

in the building of a hut on Little Green. It was opened in June of that year, and one of the speakers was Mr H Dowling, of Frome, the last local preacher to have preached in the old chapel. The site cost £100, the hut £155 and the furnishings £45. It seated 80 people. This attempt to revive Methodism in Mells failed and the chapel was converted into a bungalow.

With the conversion of Mrs Raymond Asquith to Roman Catholicism in the 1920's there was another development. In the forties an outbuilding in the Manor was converted into a chapel and regular Roman Catholic services were held there. The Parish Priest of Frome serves it, and Monsignor Ronald Knox, who spent the latter years of his life at the Manor, was a regular celebrant there. It was while living at the Manor that Ronald Knox completed his translation of the Vulgate Version of the Bible into English. One of Prebendary Horner's curates joined the Roman Church: he was Canon Ward, who built the R.C. Church in Whittox Lane, Frome in 1853.*

*This church, now known as the Old Presbytery, was built for the Irvingites. It was only later used as a Roman Catholic Church before a new church was built in Park Road in 1928

[1] S & D N & Q, 9, 72

[2] V H S, 11, 63

TIMELESSNESS IN A VILLAGE

When I was preparing to come to Mells I had occasion to ask for the keys of the Rectory from an old servant who had worked there. I was informed that young Mr Lear had taken them as he wished to have a look round his old home. It was not until sometime later that I discovered that young Mr Lear was over 70 years of age. In actual fact he was older than the old servant.

At that time there were several people who were very much alive in the minds of the older generation, and for the newcomer it was as if they had died only yesterday. Sir John and Lady Horner were still vividly remembered. Sir John died in 1927 and Lady Horner in 1940. The Misses Horner were very much alive. They had lived to be 99 years of age, dying in 1947 and 1951. They were the daughters of Prebendary Horner, who had died in 1875. George Horner, who had followed his father as Rector, and resigned the living in 1891, also lived on in the parish until 1930. One had the feeling that all these people were still alive. Then, of course, there were the rectors, William Lear and Canon Hannay. Anyone after that was too recent to mention.

Talking to a man born in Mells about the past, he said to me: "I can never understand why the reporters always go to old man Smith on the Green when they want information about Mells. I doubt whether he

Mells Post Office

The Reading Room, once The Bull public house   *K F Yeates*

came here before 1910." Actually they always went to see him because he was not only something of a character but also had a good tale to tell. He was the only person in Mells at one time allowed to keep a dog. When he arrived in the village he was informed that he must get rid of it. His answer was that he would leave the village if he could not keep the dog. He was a good blacksmith and shoeing smith and the bailiff did not wish to lose him. He kept his dog. The Rector, Mr Lear, had his terriers, but that was different.

Teddy Allwood also lived on. He was the parish jester and the last man known to have occupied the Blind House. He was in the habit of getting drunk and could not always get home. He would reach a point in Gay Street where the Relieving Officer lived, someone would spot him, call on the Officer for help and together they would carry Teddy to the Blind House to let him sleep it off.

The Misses Baynton, who were still alive when I came to the village, also helped to give a sense of timelessness. There had been Bayntons in the parish since the time of the first Elizabeth. They too lived to about 90, and could speak about the time when Rev George

Horner was the Rector. Another family who dated from the same period, the Dodimeads, had only recently left the parish. Suddenly, three historical names disappeared from Mells: Horner, Baynton and Dodimead. There are a number of families who can trace their ancestors back for a generation or two, but it is amazing how many are of recent origin. Yet many bear local names, Seviour, King, Withers, West etc, but it is difficult to claim to be a villager, if not born there. I was told of a woman who had lived in Mells for 50 years "that she dont come from these parts, she do come from Chantry." Two miles was a long way.

Mrs Raymond Asquith, now in her eighties, who lived in the Manor House when I first came to Mells in 1959, with her memories of before the First World War, of the "Souls" who frequented the Park House and later the Manor House, as well as her intimate knowledge of the history of her family, all added to the sense of the nearness of the past. Her familiarity with the names of those who have passed into history, and of a past era of gracious living, made the past live on. Other elderly people in the village, a Mrs Gould, who shared the life of the Manor for some 60 years, and a Mrs Mounty, who had lived in the village for over 80 years, had memories of a totally different world. The older men who worked in the pits remembered a world which had been real to them but is dead to us.

Mells Village from Lime Kiln Hill

Other links with a past which is fast beginning to pass away, but is still within living memory, we have from the older craftsmen. Ted Knapton still lives at the old Smithy which his father purchased from the Cornishes, while the Longs, who were still alive when I arrived in Mells, had done the plastering and tiling at Mells and Cranmore for more than a century. Geoffrey Swanton's grandfather became a church-warden nearly a century ago, and was followed by his son and grandson. There is Ted Draper, whose father came to Mells with Mr Lear in 1891 as his gardener, and who lives in the house where he was born more than 70 years ago.

Many links with the past are gone; some remain in the memory only. Percy Osborne, standing with me in the churchyard one day, said: "Many faithful servants lie buried here." Time and eternity are closely linked in a village community, and especially in one in which the Lordship of the Manor has remained in the hands of one family for some 400 years as at Mells.

"The whirr of the spinning wheels has ceased in our parlours, and we hear no more the treadles of the loom, and swift silkennoise of the flung shuttle, the intermittent thud of the batten. But the imagination hears them, and theirs is the melody of romance.

When antique things are also country things, they are easier to write about, for there is a permanence, a continuity in a country life which makes the lapse of time of little moment."[1]

[1]Mary Webb, *Precious Bane*

APPENDIX

THE SAXON BOUNDARIES OF MELLS

Reproduced from *The Saxon Charters of Somerset,* by G B
Grundy, Part IV.

by. = boundary

This was published as an appendix to the Proceedings of the
Somersetshire Archaeological and Natural History Society, vol 76,
1930, 98-101.

B 776, K 393 is a charter recording the grant of 20 hides at *Milne*
to the Earl Athelstan by King Edmund in 942.

Survey

The text of the extant survey appears to be of the earlier half of the
13th century. There is no intrinsic evidence of its being a copy of an
earlier survey.

1 *Erist of Todanbrigge* (read *Todanberghe* from landmark 16) *of
thare Muchel Dich on Mordrancombe* : 'First from Toda's Camp from
the Great Dyke to Murder Combe.'

2 *Of,* etc *on Slacombe* : 'From Murder Combe to Combe.'

The survey begins at the Mells Stream near the SE angle of the
parish. The actual point is the NW angle of Tedbury Camp, the camp
being of course the *Todanbergh* of the survey. The Great Dyke is the
western ditch of the camp, along which the parish by passes. Murder
Combe is still so called. It is that part of Whatley Bottom at the point
where the latter is crossed by the road from Frome to Mells. *Slacombe*
of 2 is Whatley Bottom along which the parish boundary passes.

3 *Of,* etc *on Boreswelle* : 'From . . . Combe to Boar's Spring.'

This was on the S by of the parish, the spring marked on OM6
about 1 fur NW of Chantry.

4 *Of,* etc *on than Merkeden Ok to Feger Ok* : 'From Boar's
Spring to the Marked Oak to Fair Oak.'
The Marked Oak was probably at the SW angle of the parish about ½ m
W of Little Elm. The Fair Oak was probably on the W by about ¼ m N
of SW angle, where the by. makes a slight bend.

5 *Thanen on Winaswelle* (read *Ineswelle* from next landmark) :
'Then to Ine's Spring (or Streamlet).'

This is the small brook which the W by. crosses at the Hare Warren, the wood which lies W of Finger Farm.

6 *Of Ineswelle on Worhanan Berghe :* 'From Ine's Streamlet to .. Barrow.'

7 *On Wolfbergh :* 'To Wolf Barrow.'

These two last landmarks were probably barrows on the high land about Melcombe Wood.

8 *Thanen on Wolfpol:* 'Then to Wolf Brook.'

This was the brook on the W by which passes through Vobster.

9 *Of,* etc *end lang stremes on Schippeburg* (read *Schipperugge) westward :* 'From Wolf Brook along the stream to the west side of Sheep Ridge.'

The old name survives in that of Shipperidge Wood, the small wood just outside the W by to the SE of Upper Vobster. There is no sign apparently of a camp on the ridge on which the wood stands and so I have amended the reading, and take the landmark to be the ridge itself.

Before reaching the ridge the by. runs for about a furlong along the *Wolfpol,* as described in the landmark.

10 *On Harenapildorewei:* 'To the Way of the Hoar Appletree.'

This was probably along the line of road on the W by which crosses that by to the E of Newbury House.

11 *There he out lit on Mereston :* 'Then it goes on to the Boundary Stone.'

This stone, as the next landmark indicates, was where the road running E from Babington Church meets the W by of the parish.

12 *Of,* etc *end lang Mereweies to Likan Trowe :* 'From the Stone along the Boundary Way to Lika's (?) Tree.'

The Boundary Way is the road which runs along the E edge of Babington Park. The by follows it till about 400 yds N of the railway.

13 *Thanen est lang Dich to Redwines Thome :* 'Then east along the Dyke to Redwin's Thorntree.'

The by., as described in the survey, now begins to run E along the N by of the parish. Along this by. the Dyke ran. The tree was evidently at the NE angle of the parish by, nearly due W of the village of Buckland Denham.

14 *Thanen on Baddanpille* : 'Then to Badda's Brook.'

15 *Of,* etc. *on Berleighe mideward* : 'From the Brook to the middle of Barrow Lea.'

Barrow Hill is marked in Buckland Denham parish E of where the railway cuts the E by. of Mells. The lea must have been close to or about the line of the railway. Various springs are marked on the hillside near this part of the E by *Baddan Pil* was probably some small brook flowing from one of them, perhaps at one of the angles in the E by. to the N of the railway.

16 *Thanen endlang Hagen on Petanberberwe* : 'then along the Hedge of the Game Enclosure to . . . Camp.'[1]

This is evidently the camp on Newbury Hill. Probably the neighbouring wood called Newbury Firs is a surviving remnant of the Game Enclosure.

17 *Thanen on tha Stanenpile:* 'Then to the Heap of Stones.'

This was where the E by. makes a short bend when it comes to Wadbury Valley.

18 *Of,* etc *eft on Todanberghe on the Muchel Dich:* 'From the Heap of Stones to Toda's Camp to the Great Dyke.'

See landmark 1.

---

[1] I fancy that the name of the camp is corrupted in the text; but I cannot amend it.

INDEX

Horner Robert 24

Horner Samuel 59

Horner Colonel Thomas 13 14 34 36 39 43 45 46 47 58 69 75 77 79

Horwood 27 81 82

Ireson 46

Kilmersdon 15 16 24 44

Knox 34 89

Lamaire 54 56

Lear 60 91 92 94

Leigh 15 16 17 26 41 50 53

Leland 9 27 35 38 64

Longleat 42

Lutyens 31 34 38 40 89

Lyttleton 33

Malte 42

McKenna 34 49

Melcombe 9 14 23 25 40

Mells Park House 13 18 33 36 37 38 40 47 49 93

Mells Road 11 66

Munnings 33

Murdercombe 9

Newbury 9 64

New Street 17 20 35 50 61 74 79 84

Nicholson 31

Nunney 25 41

Oxford & Asquith 43

Paget 29 39 46 56 59

Parsonage House 37

Poyntz. 17 38 61 77

Rectory 35 37 52 59 79

Rudhall 34

St Andrews College 48 52 81

St Dominics Chapel 88

Samuels 15 19 53

Sassoon 34

Selwood 10 12 21 22 26 35

Sherman 52

Shipperidge 25

Skinner 59 65

Singers 30

Soane 46

Stansfield 29 81 82

Talbot Inn 50

Tedbury 9

Trotter 46

Trudoxhill 25 29

Turnpike 73

Twells 83

Vennell 30

Vobster 9 23 38 49 63 64 80 87 88

Wadbury 9 40 66 74

Wesley 88

Wheatley 28 35 40 53

Whiting 40

Woadman 61

Woodlands End 14 3 35 50 88

Workhouse 50 69 70 71 74

Wrags Mill 14

Yeomanry 13 39 45